Twayne's English Authors Series

EDITOR OF THIS VOLUME

George D. Economou

Long Island University

William Dunbar

TEAS 257

WILLIAM DUNBAR

By EDMUND REISS

Duke University

TWAYNE PUBLISHERS

A DIVISION OF G. K. HALL & CO., BOSTON

Printed on permanent/durable acid-free paper and bound
in the United States of America

First Printing

Library of Congress Cataloging in Publication Data

Reiss, Edmund.
William Dunbar.

(Twayne's English authors series ; TEAS 257)
Bibliography: p. 173–76
Includes index.
1. Dunbar, William, 1460?–1520?—Criticism
and interpretation.
PR2269.R4   1979   821'.2   78-24500
ISBN 0-8057-6750-9

For
Bartlett Jere Whiting
who
"this mater coud illumynit have full brycht"

Contents

About the Author

Edmund Reiss, Professor of English at Duke University, was born in Brooklyn, New York in 1934. He received his Ph.D. degree from Harvard University and has held professorships at Western Reserve University and the Pennsylvania State University, as well as visiting professorships at Harvard and Columbia University. Along with publishing more than thirty-five articles in learned journals on medieval literature, Professor Reiss is the author of *The Art of the Middle English Lyric* (1972), *Elements of Literary Analysis* (1967), and the Twayne English Authors volume, *Sir Thomas Malory* (1966). He was founder and coeditor of the *Chaucer Review* and is now Associate Editor of the *Journal of Medieval and Renaissance Studies*. Besides being Bibliographer and Section Head of the *MLA International Bibliography*, he is the author of a forthcoming annotated bibliography, *Arthurian Legend and Romance*. He is also preparing editions for the Variorum Chaucer and the Chaucer Library, and is coeditor of the forthcoming *Complete Poetry of John Skelton*. At present, he is working on a full-length study of concepts of love in medieval thought and literature.

Preface

Even though William Dunbar has long been recognized as an accomplished master of the craft of poetry and an important link between the Middle Ages and the Renaissance, he has not been studied as much as he deserves and, indeed, needs to be. Perhaps because the end of the fifteenth and beginning of the sixteenth century is something of a no man's land in English literature, and because Dunbar's Middle Scots language is frequently difficult to understand, critical analyses of his works have been more general than particular and much fewer in number than accounts of the man and his time. The purpose of this study is to assess the nature of Dunbar's accomplishment, to understand the dominant themes and motifs running through his poetry, and to examine the meaning and merits of his various individual poems.

Although several editions of Dunbar's poetry have been prepared, many textual problems still exist. The edition followed here, that of W. Mackay Mackenzie (1932), is used only because it is the most recent and most widely available of the complete editions. Several poems once thought to be by Dunbar are now regarded as spurious, and the pieces listed by Mackenzie as attributions are ignored in this study. Even though several of these—the *Ballad of Kynd Kyttok,* the *Manere of Crying of ane Play,* and the *Freiris of Berwick*—are significant poems wholly deserving critical attention, they can only be distracting in a study aimed at understanding the nature and achievement of Dunbar's poetry. The poems discussed here are therefore taken from the eighty-four pieces listed in Mackenzie as being by Dunbar. In looking at these, I have ignored the classifications made by various editors, including Mackenzie, and have rejected the traditional titles given to the poems by modern editors. Not only are these frequently inadequate in suggesting what the poems are really about, they are too often misleading.

Chapter 1 grounds Dunbar in medieval tradition and in Middle Scots literature and shows some of the difficulties presented by his work. Chapter 2 is concerned with the autobiographical element in his poems, with seeing in particular that the narrator is not necessarily the poet. Chapter 3 focuses on the influence that the court of King James IV had on his poems. Chapter 4 examines the significance of Dunbar's being a cleric and at times an overt Christian moralist. Chapter 5 emphasizes the idea and treatment of love in his poems. Finally, chapter 6 looks at some significant patterns of imagery, as well as various poetic techniques, found throughout the verse.

I am particularly indebted to Professor B. J. Whiting of Harvard University, who many years ago introduced me to the pleasures of Middle Scots poetry and who has since been a valued critic and friend. I am also grateful to my wife Louise and my research assistant Beverly Taylor for their close reading and perceptive criticism of my typescript. I furthermore wish to thank the Research Council of Duke University for providing financial support for this study.

EDMUND REISS

Durham, North Carolina

Chronology

1504 March 17, Dunbar celebrates his first mass and receives an offering from the king.

1506 January, Dunbar receives gift of clothes from the king; gift repeated the next year. Imprisonment of Donald Owre; poem on subject apparently written by Dunbar soon afterward.

1507 June, tournament held in honor of black lady; thought to have inspired poem by Dunbar. Walter Chepman and Andrew Myllar set up first printing press in Scotland. September 27, John Damian, Abbot of Tungland attempts flight, providing occasion for two poems by Dunbar and allusion in third.

1508 May 9, Lord Bernar Stewart arrives in Scotland, only to die on June 11, both events providing occasions for poems by Dunbar. Six poems by Dunbar printed by Chepman and Myllar.

1509 Death of Henry VII; beginning of reign of Henry VIII of England.

1511 August, queen visits Aberdeen; occasion of poem by Dunbar.

1513 September 9, Battle of Flodden; defeat of Scots by English and death of James IV.

1517 June, the duke of Albany, after attempting to govern Scotland, returns to France, providing occasion for last poem attributed to Dunbar.

1522 Death of Gavin Douglas.

1529 June 21, Death of John Skelton.

1530 Sir David Lindsay writes *Testament of the Papyngo;* speaks of Dunbar as dead.

CHAPTER 1

Introduction

WILLIAM Dunbar has been called perhaps the greatest of all Scottish poets, as well as the finest lyric poet between Geoffrey Chaucer and Thomas Wyatt.[1] Writing at the turn of the sixteenth century, he may be the first significant poet in English whose corpus consists almost entirely of short and nonnarrative poems. He is also a transition figure between the Middle Ages and the Renaissance, and in appreciating his accomplishments we must do more than note how he differs from medieval tradition. Scotland in Dunbar's time was "still mediaeval, more emphatically so than the process of the century or the imminence of the Renaissance might lead us to expect."[2] It is important to see not only that his work is grounded in the Middle Ages but that his view of nature, man, and poetry is essentially medieval. Moreover, such particularly medieval poetic conventions as the dream allegory, such traditional verse forms as rhyme royal, and such standard themes as the mutability of life and the imminence of death mark his poetry.

To say that Dunbar is most properly examined as a medieval poet is not to deny his metrical experimentation—though it may be too much to say that he advanced "the technique of lyric art to a point not realized in English since the Anglo-Saxon *Wife's Lament.*"[3] It is rather to insist that Dunbar is at the end of a long tradition, and Arthur K. Moore's study of the Middle English secular lyric rightly concludes with a chapter on Dunbar.[4] On the basis of evidence found in Dunbar's own poetry, we may see that the poet saw himself as the inheritor of medieval tradition. In the famous piece known as the *Lament for the Makaris* (no. 7),[5] for instance, he links himself to twenty-four English and Scottish poets who had died, beginning with Chaucer, John Gower, and John Lydgate (50–51), the triumvirate of late medieval poets famous in the fifteenth and sixteenth centuries for having first given prestige to the English language.[6]

13

The single most important influence on Dunbar's work is without a doubt Geoffrey Chaucer, referred to by Dunbar in the *Lament* as "of makaris flour" (50) and in the *Goldyn Targe* (no. 56) as "rose of rethoris all" (253). Although Chaucer died nearly one hundred years before the bulk of Dunbar's extant poetry was written, he provided a legacy that dominated poetry in both England and Scotland until the late sixteenth century. At the same time, to describe Dunbar as a Scottish Chaucerian is to appreciate only inadequately his original genius. While the differences between the two writers are real and in most cases obvious, it is an oversimplification to say that Dunbar "is not, save in a few points, a disciple of Chaucer."[7] Comparing the two poets, C. S. Lewis makes a perceptive statement of the differences when he writes that Dunbar "lacks what is best in Chaucer and Chaucer lacks what is best in him. He is not a story-teller nor a delineator of character, and his wild whoops of laughter have little in common with Chaucer's human comedy. He has nothing of Chaucer's confiding informality—we never see him in literary undress. On the other hand, he has at his command a resonant singing voice (a voice to lift a roof with) and a goblin energy which Chaucer has not."[8] At the same time, as Denton Fox realizes, Dunbar is "immensely indebted" to Chaucer, especially in matters of technique and in choices of genre, even though the debt is not very easy to measure.[9]

To say, as James Kinsley does, that Dunbar "is an assured and independent inheritor of a European tradition far removed from Chaucer in temperament"[10] is misleading; for even if Kinsley is to be seen echoing Lewis's view that Dunbar is "the accomplished master of one tradition that goes back to *Beowulf* and of another that goes back to the Troubadours,"[11] Chaucer may have provided Dunbar with an open door to medieval traditions and conventions. And as Fox cogently points out, "Dunbar expects his readers to be acquainted with the traditional genres and themes, and to appreciate his novel rehandling of them."[12] The Chaucerian influence may also have been magnified by Dunbar's reading of John Lydgate, whose influence is to be seen not only in matters of aureate diction, the highly ornamental language that marks some of Dunbar's most significant poems,[13] but also in matters of details in a few pieces. Still, it should be stressed that Dunbar is never a close imitator of anyone, and that none of his poems is an obvious redoing of any other literary work.[14]

Besides using themes, forms, and conventions found in Middle English poetry, Dunbar clearly inherited medieval French literary traditions; but the influence is never direct. For instance, the most obvious French tradition is that stemming from the thirteenth-century *Roman de la Rose*. But this work had so permeated all parts of Western literature by the fifteenth century—part even being translated by Chaucer—that any positive direct influence is difficult to find. Also, any influence from such fourteenth-century French poets as Guillaume de Machaut, Jean Froissart, and Eustache Deschamps came by and large via Chaucer, who had used their work.[15] And although relationships may be made between Dunbar and such fifteenth-century figures as Alain Chartier, Charles d'Orleans, and, in terms of diction, the *Grands Rhétoriqueurs*, any influence is indirect rather than direct. As the aureate diction probably came mainly from Lydgate, so such French verse forms as the ballade probably came to Dunbar from the works of Chaucer and John Gower. As Janet M. Smith realizes, we cannot say definitely that any French writer had a personal influence on Dunbar. He never worked "with a foreign book at his elbow—unless perhaps it were Chaucer, who was hardly a foreigner."[16] Dunbar has also been compared often to the fifteenth-century French poet François Villon, even being called the Villon of Scotland,[17] but the two men are only superficially similar. As A. M. Kinghorn concludes after making a full comparison and contrast between their works, necessarily emphasizing the differences, Villon is "modern," whereas Dunbar is rooted in the Middle Ages.[18]

While the traditional term Scottish Chaucerian only inadequately describes Dunbar, it does serve the purpose of joining him to other Scottish writers of the late fifteenth and early sixteenth centuries—mainly Robert Henryson and Gavin Douglas—who seem likewise to have been immersed in Chaucerian writings and who together created a literature which could more than rival that being written at the time south of the river Tweed or across the English channel.[19] This "golden age of Scottish poetry," representing "a recovery, consciously made of much of the outworn artifice of the Middle Ages, which had not yet reached, or hardly reached, the northern portion of the island," produced writings generally artificial and experimental, and raised the Scottish language to a position of literary excellence.[20]

The Scottish language—as opposed to both the English spoken

elsewhere in the British Isles at the time and Scottish Gaelic, the
language of the Highlands and the Islands—developed from the
Northern dialect of Middle English in the early fifteenth century.
The term Early Scots is sometimes used to describe the language of
the Northern English romances of the late fourteenth century and
that of John Barbour's *Bruce*—the national epic of Scotland—written about 1375; but the term is, as G. G. Smith points out, "more
political than philological."[21] The related linguistic term Middle
Scots is probably best understood as a parallel to the term Middle
English. Although the *Kingis Quair*—written in the early fifteenth
century and attributed to James I of Scotland—is sometimes taken
as the beginning of Middle Scots literature, the language of this
poem, mixing Midland and Southern forms with Northern ones, can
hardly be called Scots. Middle Scots may be considered as "the
literary language of Scotland written between the latter half of the
fifteenth and the early decades of the seventeenth century."[22] It is
most meaningfully used to describe the work of Henryson, Douglas,
Dunbar, and the sixteenth-century poet Sir David Lindsay.

Whereas these poets shared essentially the same language, national heritage, and medieval–Chaucerian background, they wrote
quite different kinds of poetry. Although stylistic virtuosity is a
keynote of this poetry, Dunbar stands out both as the best poet and
as the one most at home in all forms of poetry, though at the same
time he is said to be "the most representative of the essential quality
of Middle Scots poetry."[23] In fact, no poet writing in English—or
Scots—before Dunbar had expressed himself "in such a diversity of
metres." For all his medieval grounding "he does not hesitate to
alter and adapt, and he justifies his audacity by the felicity of his
experiments."[24] Whether the new in Dunbar is stronger or more
meritorious than the old is moot, and while his verse stands out by
virtue of its brevity from the bulk of fifteenth-century poetry, it is
likewise different from such early Renaissance lyrics as those by
Wyatt and the earl of Surrey. Superficially at least, Dunbar is probably most like his exact English contemporary John Skelton; but to
subordinate one to the other—to call Dunbar the Scottish Skelton,
for instance—is inadequate and misleading.[25]

The range of Dunbar's poetry is phenomenal, and his ability to
use different forms and styles striking; as Lewis says, "all his effects
are calculated and nearly all are successful."[26] Although several
attempts to classify his verse have been made—all of which are

inadequate—that made by A. J. G. Mackay in the introduction to the Scottish Text Society edition of Dunbar may serve to illustrate something of the variety represented by the eighty-five or so poems now accepted as comprising the Dunbar canon: allegorical poems, narrative poems or tales, amatory or love poems, comic or humorous poems, laudatory poems or panegyrics, vituperative poems or invectives, precatory poems or petitions to the king or queen, satirical poems, moral poems, religious poems or hymns.[27] Even allowing for overlapping, the sheer variety must strike a reader as impressive, as must the varied stanzaic forms. Dunbar's poems are in stanzas of four, five, six, seven, eight, twelve, and sixteen lines, as well as in rhyming couplets and in long alliterative lines.

Perhaps because of this range and virtuosity, it is difficult to talk meaningfully about what Dunbar is like as a poet or about how his poetry causes us to respond. His verse is protean, hard to hold securely with confidence that any particular piece represents the "real" Dunbar more than does any other piece. For instance, Mackay writes that Dunbar "is one of the poets of reflection, not one of the poets of passion";[28] but Lewis cautions us, "If you like tones and nuances you will not enjoy Dunbar; he will deafen you."[29] Although these two evaluations are not necessarily contradictory, they are sufficiently opposed to make us wonder whether the two critics are describing the same poet. Readers will naturally prefer poems of one sort to others, but even the best-intentioned reader may not feel comfortable with the variety of the Dunbar offering and may have difficulty defining what is most typical of Dunbar. Denton Fox makes a good presentation of the problem:

One of the most surprising things about Dunbar is that he wrote so many different sorts of poetry: scatological abuse, the stiffest and most bejewelled panegyric, and everything in between. Scholars have tried to sort out his poetry by periods, with a frivolous youth and a pious old age, but there is no evidence to support this, and a good deal to contradict it. One might as well postulate an afternoon Dunbar, who wrote formal and ceremonial verse, an evening Dunbar, who wrote bawdry in the taverns, and a morning-after Dunbar, who wrote moral lyrics and petitions for money. The truth, of course, is simply that Dunbar wrote happily and skilfully in almost any genre.[30]

It is as unsatisfactory to state, say, that Dunbar is basically a court poet and, after singling out the poems that fit into this category, to subordinate all the other poems to these, as it would be to go through the *Canterbury Tales* to define which kind of tale is most representative of Chaucer.

To look at Dunbar's corpus of poems in terms of sets of dichotomies—for instance, moralizings opposed to petitions, bawdy tales opposed to religious hymns—is just as inadequate. To proceed on the assumption that one kind of poem is *de facto* superior to or more significant than another kind of poem is just as bad. The prejudice that seriousness and gravity go properly and necessarily hand in hand is a modern not a medieval one; and as we may tend to think that a humorous poem like Chaucer's *Miller's Tale* is necessarily less serious than a courtly romance like his *Knight's Tale*, so we may feel that Dunbar's overtly humorous poems are trivial, at least more so than his overtly grave ones, even though, if length is any kind of criterion for significance, the two longest poems in his canon, the *Tretis of the Tua Mariit Wemen and the Wedo* and the *Flyting of Dunbar and Kennedie*, are notably humorous and bawdy.

Even when we try to classify Dunbar in terms of a particular genre, several problems exist; for we must realize, as Mackay does, that "beneath the humourist in Dunbar there was the moralist always, and at times the preacher."[31] Although several of his poems are properly classified as satires, he is "not a satirist in any formal sense"; moreover, "his work embodies less of the purely conventional and shows greater originality, than that of any other satirical writer of his time."[32] Reading one poem by Dunbar does not necessarily prepare us for reading another; each is, as it were, *sui generis*; and the sincerity of one piece should not hinder us from appreciating the irony of the next.

Although Dunbar can hardly be called a narrative poet, to say, as Moore does, that he "has nothing of the steady detachment necessary to the accomplishment of extensive narrative"[33] is misleading, since we have no extensive narratives from his pen. Instead of analyzing his actual accomplishments, this critical evaluation predicts in effect that if we had such pieces from Dunbar, we would see a lack of steady detachment. And if anything is apparent in the reading of this poet, it is that he is beyond the predictable. The fact that Dunbar chose to write short poems instead of extensive narratives does not mean that he was necessarily unable to express himself in the traditional narrative forms that came to him from the

Middle Ages. Dunbar's interest was in sound, rhythm, patterns of language, indeed in all the "colours" of poetry; and he did not feel the need to couch these in narrative frames.

It is likewise difficult to know how much Dunbar should be regarded as a lyric poet. If relatively short pieces are automatically lyrics, then Dunbar is a lyric poet. But if we wish to make the term more meaningful and limit the genre to, say, those poems showing, in Moore's phrase, "purely individual expression,"[34] some unexpected problems develop; for Dunbar as a medieval poet seems to be expressing directly and indirectly the accepted truths and values of his religion, not any particular personal notions, as well as the traditional themes of medieval poetry, not his own special concerns. Dunbar, as far as we know, was a "public" poet; that is, he wrote by and large for an immediate audience. And even though his poems may not be "entirely, or indeed pre-eminently, occasional in character,"[35] he was still not using the lyric as a vehicle for expressing his own emotions or even his own philosophy of life. He was no William Wordsworth or John Keats, and the notion of poetry as "a spontaneous overflow of powerful feelings," based on "emotion recollected in tranquility" is totally foreign to him. If we avoid emphasizing subjective response, however, and consider lyrics as essentially nonnarrative poems exhibiting musical qualities, then we may conclude that Dunbar has without a doubt written lyrics, even when they are couched in the forms of petitions, essays, and satires.

In Dunbar's poetry the writer takes many roles and offers many poses, none of which may be a mirror image of himself. Dunbar is a craftsman, a professional poet, whether or not poetry was his vocation. A fact generally ignored, but one that may be significant, is that Dunbar may not have written a single poem—at least none of those that are extant—before he was in his forties; moreover, the bulk of his poetry was composed after he was ordained as a cleric. The two most obvious voices of Dunbar—"one given to pasquinade and the other to panegyric"[36]—are intentional and equally contrived. Whether aureate, that is, pointedly eloquent and highly ornamental, or "eldritch," that is, wild, exuberant, and grotesque, Dunbar was conscious of the effects he was creating. Nothing in his poetry is accidental, and even what has been termed his "restless and nervous force" is used purposefully.[37] Comparing him with John Skelton, whose effects seem accidental, Lewis writes that "In a

poem by Skelton anything may happen, and Skelton has no more
notion than you what it will be." His charm is that of the amateur,
whereas Dunbar is "professional through and through"; we can be
sure that "the last line of each poem was in view before he wrote the
first."[38]

Even though the effect of Dunbar's poetry is occasionally one of
overstatement or grossness, his humor, really a "delight in the
whimsical," is "more often subtle than blatant, a mirthfulness of the
eye rather than of the throat."[39] And although the separation between the eldritch and the aureate voices is great, it is "not so great
that they are ever really disconnected."[40] Similarly, the dichotomies
we sense as we read through Dunbar's eighty-four poems are finally
more apparent than real and more of our making than of the poet's.

Still, we tend to find Dunbar a difficult poet to read and appreciate, not just because of his occasionally strange vocabulary; and
his position in the process of late fifteenth- and early sixteenth-century poetry is likewise difficult to define. As G. G. Smith states, "his
originality rather defies the interpretation of his work in relation to
that of more even-tenored, if less brilliant, contemporaries. He is
strangely complex, at once conventional and audacious; yet he
makes no compromise between these opposites, but throws them
together in daring contrast."[41]

CHAPTER 2

The Poet and the Narrator

I The Biographical Evidence

ONE of the main difficulties with Dunbar's poetry is that so much of it seems personal, and, indeed, it has most frequently been regarded as a main source for his life, filling out the little that is positively known about the man. As W. Mackay Mackenzie states of Dunbar's life story, it "is almost a blank. What has been written of it, with more or less confidence, is to a large extent conjecture."[1] The only indisputable evidence is little indeed. It is clear that Dunbar was associated with the court of the Scottish king James IV: according to the Privy Seal Register he received a pension of ten pounds from the king in 1500, to be paid to him "for al the dais of his life," or until he should receive a benefice worth forty pounds a year.[2] In 1507, according to the accounts of the Lord High Treasurer of Scotland, the amount was increased to twenty pounds and in 1510 to eighty pounds, until he should be promoted to a benefice worth one hundred pounds per year.

In addition, the treasurer's accounts show that in December, 1501, Dunbar was paid a sum "efter he com furth of Ingland"—an entry that, coupled with the reference in Henry VII's Privy Purse expenses for December, 1501, and January, 1502, to the "Rhymer of Scotland," has led some scholars to believe that he was associated with the embassy that completed the treaty for the marriage of James with Margaret Tudor.[3] It is also recorded that Dunbar received additional money in January, 1506, "be the Kingis command, for caus he wantit his goun at 3ule," that is, apparently, funds for the purchase of new clothes at Christmas, a gift repeated the next year.

In 1504, a notation appears that the king made an offering at "Maister William Dunbar's first mes," showing that by at least this date Dunbar was a priest as well as a court poet and possibly a civil servant. This William Dunbar may be the one who received a degree of determinant, or bachelor of arts, from St. Andrews University in 1477, and the degree of licentiate, or master of arts, in 1479.[4]

The last entry about Dunbar in the treasurer's accounts is for 14 May, 1513, and notes that his pension has been paid. The accounts for the next two years are not preserved, due largely to the disruption of the Scottish government caused by the war with England and the disastrous Battle of Flodden in September, 1513; but when entries begin again, in June, 1515, no further reference is made to Dunbar or to his pension. It would seem either that the payments had lapsed—James had been killed at Flodden—or that the poet had at last received a benefice, or that he was dead. Although some commentators would like to think that he died at Flodden, evidence that he was alive in 1517 is provided by events referred to in the poem "Thow that in hevin, for our salvatioun (no. 65)."[5] If he was still alive then, he was definitely dead by 1530; for in that year, at the beginning of his *Testament of the Papyngo*, Sir David Lindsay includes a lament for dead Scottish poets including Dunbar.[6] The remaining details of Dunbar's life have been supplied from the poems, although full "biographies" may be found in A. J. G. Mackay's introduction to the Scottish Text Society edition of Dunbar's poems,[7] and, more recently, in J. W. Baxter's *William Dunbar. A Biographical Study* (1952).

We have a notion of the date of Dunbar's birth only because of a line in *The Flyting of Dunbar and Kennedie* (no. 6), "Thou was consavit [conceived] in the grete eclips" (489), taken as referring to the eclipse on 18 July, 1460, a date which would most likely place the poet's birth early in 1461. Although this may seem to be "a very suitable date,"[8] the possibility exists that Kennedy may simply have been connecting Dunbar's origin abusively with an unpleasant occurrence.[9] Few modern readers have taken at face value Kennedy's insult that Dunbar was a foundling (38); they have, however, responded more positively to Kennedy's associating him with the treacherous earls of Dunbar (262)—though not, it should be noted, to Kennedy's assertion that Dunbar's family descended from the union of a she-bear and a devil (259). Similarly, Kennedy's calling him a "dirtfast dearch" (33) and a "myten" (494), both nouns meaning dwarf, has caused some scholars to infer that Dunbar was "of short stature";[10] but no one has taken literally Kennedy's fuller description of his as "Wod werwoif, worme, and scorpion vennemous" (251). The problem is not just how to view Kennedy's insults and accusations—if indeed the parts of the *Flyting* attributed to Walter Kennedy are by him and not by Dunbar himself—it is, more, how to view what Dunbar says about himself in his various poems.

In "This nycht, befoir the dawing cleir" (no. 4),[11] for example, after the spirit purporting to be St. Francis appears to the poet and tells him that he should become a friar, Dunbar responds, "Gif [if] evir my fortoun wes to be a freir,/ The dait thairof is past full mony a yeir"; for in the past he had travelled in friars' garb throughout England and Piccardy, deceiving in "the freiris style" (31–45). On the basis of this evidence scholars have concluded that Dunbar had been for a time a novice of the Franciscan order of friars,[12] though few readers have taken seriously the accusation in the *Flyting* that Dunbar had gone about the Scottish Lowlands as a pardoner (425–26) or that he had gone into France as an "unhonest" pilgrim (430–32). Biographical critics, more, it would seem, than nature, abhor a vacuum and endeavor to fill one as readily and as best they can.

II *The Author in His Poems*

There is no question that Dunbar puts himself in his poems, even by name, as in the *Flyting* and in the so-called *Dance in the Quenis Chalmer* (no. 32),[13] where, after describing the performances of various members of the king's household, the poet writes of himself:

> Than cam in Dunbar the Mackar;
> On all the flure thair was nane frackar [more active],
> And thair he dancet the dirrye dantoun;
> He hoppet lyk a pillie wanton [lively colt (?)],
>   For luff of Musgraeffe, men tellis me;
> He trippet, quhill he tint his panton [lost his slipper]:
>   A mirrear dance mycht na man se.
>
> (22–28)

The picture of Dunbar here is certainly to be contrasted with those given earlier in the poem of "lumbering old courtiers shuffling round,"[14] but it is misleading to see in this description "a trait of the poet's character—his great animal spirit and love of fun"[15] or to take the details at face value and to conclude, for instance, that Dunbar is actually in love with Mistress Musgrave, whoever she might be.[16] In a sense Dunbar does what Chaucer did when he included himself as a character on the Canterbury pilgrimage. For all its realistic language and detail, the picture here is essentially without verisimilitude; or, rather, to look for verisimilitude is to fail to see properly that the whole dance is a study in the incongruous and, probably, the ridiculous. The refrain, "A mirrear dance mycht na man see," is hardly a meaningful description of this dance; terms like "sillier" and "stranger" would describe the event far more accurately than "mirrear."

The dance has in effect no reality beyond itself; it is the poem. Beginning without any preliminaries, "Sir Jhon Sinclair begowthe [began] to dance," the work ends when "the Quenis Dog"[17] joins the dance, moving about "mastevlyk" and stinking "lyk a tyk" (47–48). The seven stanzas of the poem are more a series of cameos than a progressing narrative or a developing picture. What do increase in the course of the poem are an awareness of the physical, even of the bestial, and an interplay of sensory details. Animal imagery runs throughout the piece: one dancer staggers like a stumbling cart horse ("ane strummall aver," 11); another is like a young ox ("stirk," 17) staggering in the rye; Dunbar is like a colt; and the culmination of this imagery is the use of canine terms in the last stanza.

Shouts and laughter from the audience mingle, moreover, with bodily sounds emitted inadvertently by the dancers—it is said of one dancer, for instance, that "His hippis gaff mony hoddous cry" (18)—as they stagger and jump around, and reinforce the descriptive language used by the poet—the same dancer is called "ane hommiltye jommeltye juffler" (16). The final participation by "the Quenis Dog" provides both the culmination of the sensory details—especially those of smell—and of the ludicrous. Running throughout the work, continuing the emphasis on the physical, is the suggestion of sexual activity implicit in the dance itself, especially if, as the colophon of the poem in the Maitland manuscript states, its location is in a bedroom, even the queen's chamber. More specifically, the "dirrye dantoun" (24) danced by Dunbar seems to be the same as the "dery dan" performed by the two lovers in "In secreit place this hyndir nycht" (no. 28),[18] a dance that is an obvious, and probably humorous, sexual euphemism.

The characters here—including Dunbar—are subordinate to the

act of the dance and function as real people only insofar as they serve to create the impression of the incongruous.[19] They are like "the Quenis Dog" and "Dame Dounteboir" (36)—a name signifying a lady in waiting, sometimes having "a comic and lascivious nuance"[20]—in being ultimately more metaphorical than realistic. If this poem is the "write-up of an actual dance,"[21] Dunbar has seen its humorous potential and taken the event from the realm of the actual to that of the fantastic. In such a context Dunbar's presentation of himself or of his own feelings can hardly be taken seriously. When he sees Mistress Musgrave dance, he says, "Than, for hir saek, I wissitt to be/ The grytast erle or duk in France" (33–34). These lines function more as comic exaggeration than as a confession of the poet's sincere amorous yearnings.[22]

In like manner it is necessary to reevaluate what to do with a "personal" poem like *On His Heid-Ake* (no. 3), which is short enough to be quoted in full:

> My heid did yak yester nicht,
> This day to mak [write] that I na micht,
>   So sair the magryme [migraine] dois me menyie [torment],
>   Perseing my brow as ony ganyie, [arrow]
> 5 That scant I luik may on the licht.
>
> And now, schir, laitlie, eftir mes, [Mass]
> To dyt [write] thocht I begowthe to dres,
>   The sentence lay full evill till find,
>   Unsleipit in my heid behind,
> 10 Dullit in dulnes and distres.
>
> Full oft at morrow I upryse,
> Quhen that my curage [mind] sleipeing lyis,
>   For mirth, for menstrallie and play,
>   For din nor danceing nor deray, [amusement]
> 15 It will nocht walkin me no wise.

Though apparently a slight piece, it has been valued as defining the personality of the poet and has been termed "one of the earliest and most intimate of intimate poems in the Scottish language."[23] The poem has been seen as especially personal,[24] as Dunbar's "direct and unaffected apology to the King" for not managing to compose something he had promised,[25] even as a serious comment on his health, "the work of a sick man."[26]

The premise of all these views is that the subject of Dunbar's poem is actually a headache, but the title *On His Heid-Ake* comes, like most of the titles commonly given to Dunbar's poems, from Laing's 1834 edition.[27] To be precise, however, the headache is alluded to only in the first stanza and is actually most applicable only to this part of the poem. In stanza 2 the poet complains of "dulnes," that is, torpidity; and in stanza 3, he emphasizes that although his body awakens, his "curage"—here mind or strength—remains asleep. Dunbar is clearly doing more than complaining about a headache or talking about his head, though he does refer to two parts of the head. In the first stanza he stresses the ache in the front of the head—the "magryme" described as "perseing my brow" (4)—and in the second stanza he emphasizes that in spite of his intention, his "sentence" (8)—that is, his thought, or, more accurately, the matter that is of greatest significance—lies dulled "in my heid behind" (9).

The references here are to the traditional medieval division of the brain into three cells—the front one being the place of Fantasy, the middle one of Reason, and rear one of Memory. A common affliction of the front cell was known as *mania*, called "manye" in Chaucer's *Knight's Tale* and associated there with "the loveris maladye/ of Hereos."[28] And indeed Dunbar's description of his "magryme," which pierces his brow like an arrow ("ganyie," 4), seems to be more than a casual image. Cupid's arrows, in medieval tradition commonly striking the victim through the eyes, not only can cause metaphorical blindness, that is, loss of rationality—Dunbar writes, "scant I luik may on the licht" (5)—they may also result in the lover's being in a confused state of mind. Arcite in the *Knight's Tale*, after falling in love and then losing sight of his beloved, shows the ravages of this mania; and both he and the speaker in Dunbar's poem seem closely related to the narrator of Chaucer's *Book of the Duchess*, who, "for defaute of slep," takes "no kep / Of nothing," who has "felynge in nothyng," and who is "a mased thyng." This narrator describes his condition further: "Defaute of slep and hevynesse / Hath sleyn my spirit of quyknesse / That I have lost al lustyhede. / Suche fantasies ben in myn hede,/ So I not what is best to doo."[29] Not that Dunbar is necessarily writing about the state of love, though love as one form of involvement in worldly pleasure may be pertinent to this poem. Whatever the cause, the disease of both Dunbar's speaker and Chaucer's figures would seem to be mania, even melancholia.

Dunbar's speaker says that his head aches so much that he was not able to write ("mak," 2), that, although he tried to "dyt" (7), the "sentence" remained within him not able to be brought into being: "The sentence lay full evill till find, / Unsleipit in my heid behind, / Dullit in dulness and distres" (8–10). The speaker finds that none of the ordinary pleasures of the world can help him—not mirth, minstrelsy, play, "din," dancing, or "deray." Worst of all, his condition is apparently not an unusual one—it occurs "Full oft at morrow" (11). "Unsleipit" in this passage presents a problem not previously noted. If it means "unasleep," as has commonly been understood,[30] there exists a difficulty in the sense of the passage. If the "sentence" is indeed unasleep, that is, awake, it is in direct contrast with the narrator's "curage" that "sleipeing lyis" (12), although the two terms would seem to be related. Although "unsleipit" may be taken to mean "unrested" or "not having slept,"[31] thereby associating the narrator's predicament with the insomnia common to such a condition—as in Chaucer's *Book of the Duchess*—such a reading is inconsistent with the final stanza of the poem. Perhaps the word should be something like "unshaped," notwithstanding problems of orthography, or, more justifiably, "onsleipit" or "ansleipit," that is, "asleep." Such a state is understandable if the "sentence" has been "Dullit in dulnes and distres."

Far from revealing a private discomfort or illness, the poem is wholly within a long medieval tradition that sees physical illness and discomfort as reflections of man's essential spiritual condition. Far from representing an actual malady to be taken literally, the headache, the dullness, and the sleepiness would surely have been regarded by Dunbar's audience as details to be viewed symbolically. Moreover, far from responding sympathetically to the speaker's complaint, this audience would have realized, first, that the speaker was no more Dunbar than the narrator of the *Book of the Duchess* was Chaucer, and, second, that the malady was more deserving of laughter than of pity. They would know that this is ultimately a humorous poem and not a sentimental one.

Dunbar is here most obviously playing with paradox: he presents a poet writing a wholly controlled poem on the subject of not being able to write. Throughout it are various contrasts—between night and morning, sleeping and waking, pain and pleasure, and past, present, and future—reflecting the intellectual manipulation going on. All of these contrasts exist as expressions of the incongruous situation of the "makar" as victim, as someone lacking even the clarity of vision of any ordinary man. For the poet to bring up mirth, minstrelsy, and play as apparent remedies for his dulled "sentence," as ways of reviving his sleeping "curage," is for him to show the extent of his confusion. Traditionally the irreconcilable opposites of the spirit, these pleasures of the flesh could only make matters worse. And indeed, in his ambiguous syntax in the final stanza, Dunbar may be suggesting precisely this point. His "curage sleipeing lyis, / For mirth, for menstrallie and play, / For din. . . ." That is, his "curage" is dormant *because of* these worldly pleasures. They have so dulled him that not even Mass is sufficient to revive him (6–8).[32]

Just as the poem is about more than a headache, so is it more than an apology to the king for being unable to write—we may even wonder whether it actually "proves" Dunbar's "position and employment as a court poet."[33] It is, rather, a witty contrast between the activity of the poet, whose "sentence" and "curage" must necessarily be awake, and that of the world—perhaps more exactly that of the king's court—whose pleasures can only dull one and keep him from looking on the light. Dunbar's originality here is in taking traditional material and, using the image of sickness, writing a poem full of moral "sentence" without giving the impression of moralizing. As with the previous poem's handling of the dance, this one does not go beyond the narrator's statement of his own physical condition. Dunbar does not give a further stanza—as he could have—suggesting the remedy for this condition. Such a *moralitas* is clear but implicit in the poem without need to be stated.

Other "personal" complaints of Dunbar may be likewise viewed as pieces of literary artistry that use references to the author and his feelings as but a way of getting into the poem. Such a reading is especially to the point in "In to thir dirk and drublie dayis (no. 10)"[34] where Nature denies the poet "all curage . . . Off sangis, ballattis, and of playis" (4–5). Again his "dule spreit" (8) is vexed with "havie thocht" (12) and his heart perishes "for languor" (9). The condition described here may be seen as precisely that of "My heid did yak yester nicht," though again commentators have taken it literally in terms of the poet's awareness of old age.[35]

A comparable heaviness of spirit is to be found in the famous poem of Dunbar's frequently referred to as the *Lament for the Makaris* (no. 7), where in the first stanza the narrative "I" laments his condition:

> I that in heill wes and gladnes,
> Am trublit now with gret seiknes,
> And feblit with infermite;
>> *Timor mortis conturbat me.*

(1–4)

Although the next several stanzas speak of the condition referred to here in terms that are general and entirely apart from the "I," editors have, apparently wholly on the basis of this first stanza, attached a title to the poem, *Quhen he wes sek.*[36] This stanza, along with the penultimate stanza, in which Dunbar says that since death has taken all his fellow poets, he knows he must necessarily be its next victim—"On forse I man his nyxt pray be" (95), has also been interpreted as providing evidence that Dunbar was in advanced age, indeed in his final years, when he wrote the poem.[37] If not on the verge of death, at least, so the common opinion goes, Dunbar must have been ill, and "from the very tone of the poem," this illness "was clearly a grave one."[38] Tom Scott not only accepts this projected illness as a fact, he makes it the basis for his interpretation of the poem: "It is odd that little attention has been paid to the chief key to the poem—the fact that Dunbar wrote it 'Quhen he wes seik.' It is not his normal vision of life that we are getting, but the vision of a man whose vitality has been lowered." [39] Although Scott recognizes that the poem uses "traditional material," specifically in its emphasis on mutability, he prefers to think that Dunbar has focused on "some specific private experience," and that this provided the impetus for his use of traditional material.[40] It is as though Scott and other commentators feel a need to rescue the *Lament* from the traditional and the conventional. If they can have it "personal," it thereby becomes something special; but there is no evidence for seeing in Dunbar's "greit seiknes" (2) anything other than the ordinary condition of man, especially that of man who has taken pleasure in temporalia. It is, in effect, the sickness described in "My heid did yak yester nicht."

The second stanza emphasizes the transitoriness of life:

> Our plesance heir is all vane glory,
> This fals warld is bot transitory,
> The flesche is brukle [brittle], the Fend is sle;
>> *Timor mortis conturbat me.*

(5–8)

The third stanza expands on this theme of mutability by presenting
it as the ordinary state of this world:

> The stait of man dois change and vary,
> Now sound, now seik, now blith, now sary,
> Now dansand mery, now like to dee;
>   *Timor mortis conturbat me.*

(9–12)

This is precisely the point illustrated by the first-person reference in
stanza 1: it is not only that the speaker is "trublit now with gret
seiknes, / And feblit with infermite" (2–3), but that he "in heill *wes*
and gladnes" (1). The insecurity resulting from the change and variance—from not being able to count on any permanence in this
world—is what is most frustrating to man; and this is the real subject
of the poem, as Dunbar writes in stanza 4:

> No stait in erd heir standis sickir;
> As with the wynd wavis the wickir [willow],
> Wavis this warldis vanite;
>   *Timor mortis conturbat me.*

(13–16)

The movement is from the particular feelings of the individual to
the general state of mankind, to the state of nature and of the world;
and, ironically, the only thing constant in all this movement is the
haunting refrain, "Fear of death confounds me," from the Office for
the Dead.[41] The "personal" assertions are best seen as part of a
rhetorical tradition. To say this is not to ignore the possibility that
the efficient cause of the poem was some particular occasion—just as
"Sir Jhon Sinclair begowthe to dance" and "My heid did yak yester
nicht" may have had their origins in some particular occasion—but,
if anything, the occasion for "I that in heill wes and gladnes" was
most likely the sickness not of Dunbar but of his fellow poet Walter
Kennedy. At the end of his list of "makaris" who have died,[42] Dunbar writes of Kennedy:

> Gud Maister Walter Kennedy
> In poynt of dede lyis veraly,
> Gret reuth it wer that so suld be;
>   *Timor mortis conturbat me.*

(89–92)

While Dunbar's sadness is surely genuine, this sadness is not the subject of his poem, and it is wrong to see the piece providing evidence for the poet's life and state of health.

III *The Poet as Poser*

Another poem, the so-called *Complaint to the King aganis Mure* (no. 5), provides a striking illustration of how biographically oriented scholarship may have caused a serious misreading of Dunbar's poetry. The poem begins with what seems to be a real and legitimate complaint by the poet: "Schir, I complane off injuris: / A refing sonne off rakyng Muris /Hes magellit [mangled] my making, throw his malis" (1–3). The poem goes on to state how this culprit has not only "dismemberit" Dunbar's "meter" (8), but has also put all sorts of cruel slander and lies (12–13), even treason (17), into Dunbar's poems. He is a fool, says the poet; he should be punished for his "deid culpabile" (22); and "sum remeid" should be given to the injured party, Dunbar (28).[43]

For centuries, from at least John Pinkerton's 1786 edition of Dunbar, readers have searched for Mure, the dastardly plagiarist who had the nerve to corrupt Dunbar's poems and who called up the righteous wrath of the poet.[44] Mackay, for instance, in his "Historical Notices of Persons Alluded to in Dunbar's Poems," an appendix to the introduction of the 1893 Scottish Text Society edition of Dunbar, writes of Mure: "It has not been discovered who this poet was who had dared to tamper with Dunbar's verses. But . . . he was probably a worthless and envious bard who used this means to get Dunbar into trouble with the Lords he represented him as satirizing."[45] By 1966, the Mure matter is still not cleared up; and Scott is puzzled even to the point of ungrammaticalness: "There is no evidence that any of the kind of slanderous gossip in verse which he complains of being interpolated into his work by Mure having come down to us" [*sic*].[46] In Scott's view Dunbar, wanting "redress against a courtier" who has marred his poetry, has penned "what must be the most original complaint ever made to any king by a poet."[47] Florence Ridley continues in this vein, writing in 1973 that "The poem suggests something of Dunbar's position at court: evidently his poetry was popular enough to be plagiarized, and he himself in sufficient favor to expect protection for it from the king."[48] Mure thus continues to exist, at least in the minds of commentators, although no one has yet discovered who he was and although there is no evidence in the extant poems of how he slandered Dunbar.

A likelihood which apparently has not occurred to anyone is that there may be no Mure, that the "refing sonne off rakyng Muris," cited in the first stanza may really be "a thieving son of the grasping Moors," moors, or blackamoors, being at the time a term of contempt. Such name-calling would be in accord with Dunbar's method later in the poem when he calls the culprit "That Cuddy Rig, the Drumfres fuill" (24). He is not saying that the culprit *is* Cuddy Rig—perhaps the name of a court fool—but that he is like a fool. The names of Mure and Cuddy Rig would both thus function metaphorically. A further possibility is that "Muris" may be a reference to the moors, the wastelands, perhaps those of Scotland.[49] If this is the case, Dunbar may be referring to the culprit as a Scotsman; and, if indeed the culprit is a creation of the poet, he may well be the poet himself. To view "Muris" in this way is to see the poem as a tongue-in-cheek complaint, one saying that the poet should not be held responsible for awkwardnesses of language and meter, or for any slander in his poems. Dunbar's pose may be compared to Chaucer's, when, at the beginning of the *Canterbury Tales* he says that any offensive plain speech should be blamed on the character whose words Chaucer is repeating, not on the poet himself.[50] The "blameth nat me" ploy, where the author detaches himself from his possibly offensive material, is part of a long literary tradition, appearing in the late Middle Ages in such major works as Jean de Meun's *Roman de la Rose*[51] and Giovanni Boccaccio's *Decameron*.[52]

No matter whether an actual occurrence was the basis for this poem, Dunbar would hardly seem to be serious in it. Couplets like "That fulle dismemberit hes my meter, / And poysonid it with strang salpeter" (8–9) are apt to cause a smile and hardly justify Baxter's comment that the tone in this poem "is not that of one who jests,"[53] or J. Schipper's that the poem "is perfectly serious and has nothing of the joke in it,"[54] or Moore's, that the poet here is "angry."[55] And the humor is heightened if the criticism is ultimately to be seen turning back on Dunbar himself, if, that is, Dunbar in an oblique *mea culpa* is presenting himself as a fool, without "wit and ressoun," lacking only "a rowndit heid" (19–20). As a comic criticism of the poet's own work, this poem may be seen in the tradition of Chaucer's Introduction to the *Man of Law's Tale*[56] and his interruption of the *Tale of Sir Thopas*.[57] In these works, however, Chaucer had put criticism of his writings in the mouths of his characters—the Man of Law and the Host; here Dunbar criticizes his work by acting as though the "offensive" parts of it are the work of another writer. The point of the two writers is the same; the difference lies in the method.

Using the pose of a petitioner to the king asking for redress against injuries, Dunbar has written a witty, sophisticated lyric. Its form—the octosyllabic seven-line stanza rhyming *aabbcbc*, with a refrain—has, as Scott notes, "satiric and comic potentialities," which Dunbar exploits.[58] And in all the other four pieces employing this form[59] Dunbar's humor and wit are obvious. Nor do any of these poems exist as "personal" utterances. Whereas the "Muris" poem (which should be called "Schir, I complayne of injuris") may not be one of Dunbar's best, it is interesting—like the *Flyting*—for its command of language and humorous invective, and certainly does not merit Scott's criticism that it is "too personal to be of much value."[60]

Both this poem and "My heid did yak yester nicht" are apparently addressed to James IV—both pieces call on a "schir," and the "Muris" poem twice has the line "Your Grace beseik I of remeid" (14, 21). These two poems are linked to ten or so other works of Dunbar likewise ostensibly addressed to the king, and asking, directly or indirectly, for relief of some sort, generally for money, clothing, or benefices. Usually classified as petitions,[61] these poems are at times obviously sincere—that is, it seems clear that Dunbar really wants what he is asking for—but at other times they are just as obviously humorous and ironic, suggesting that the request should not be taken at face value—as in the "Muris" piece.[62] Indeed, as "begging-poems," these fit into a traditional genre with a long history, in the late Middle Ages containing notable poems by Chaucer, Thomas Hoccleve, and Lydgate in English, as well as by Machaut, Froissart, and Deschamps in French—and in all of these the "sincerity" of the poet is at least suspect.[63]

When, at the end of "Complane I wald, wist I quhome till" (no. 19),[64] Dunbar writes,

> Thairfoir, O Prince maist honorable!
> Be in this meter merciabill,
> And to auld servandis haff ane E [eye]
> That lang hes lipinit [trusted] into the,

(67–70)

there can be little doubt of his seriousness. This complaint, in which he asks for justice and mercy from the king, begins with his saying that he does not know to whom he can complain—to God, to the Virgin, or "unto wardlie prince heir downe, / That dois for justice weir a crownne" (7–8)—of the "wrangis" and the "gryt injuris" that "nobillis" and "men of vertew and cuning" have long endured (9–11). For all their loyalty, love, and long service (14), these good men gain nothing from the court. Instead, rewarded ahead of them are ignoble and undeserving creatures of all kinds:

> Bot fowll, jow-jowrdane-hedit jevellis,
> Cowkin-kenseis, and culroun kevellis;
> Stuffettis, strekouris, and stafische strummellis;
> Wyld haschbaldis, haggarbaldis, and hummellis;
> Druncartis, dysouris, dyvowris, drevellis,
> Misgydit memberis of the devellis.
>
> (15–20)[65]

And so the poem goes, listing "Evill horrible monsteris, fals and fowll" (27) and piling up abusive epithets for most of its seventy-six lines until the sober petition to the king at the end.

One might well see the "bitterness" here as genuine,[66] but wonder whether it represents Dunbar's complaint about personal neglect as much as his statement of the way of the world. As the medieval ballade traditionally concluded with a petition for assistance,[67] so the "begging-poem" necessarily includes a personal element. Dunbar goes on to say that even though the king's "danger" (offishness) injures the poet, he knows that "eftir danger cumis grace" (74–75). The tone of this ending, the "muted, somewhat hopeful note,"[68] might appear out of accord with the "bitterness" seen earlier. And so it would if "Complane I wald" were viewed as an emotional *cri du coeur*.[69] On the other hand, as G. G. Smith has suggested, the poem may represent "an exercise in fifteenth-century nonsense," such as a medieval Lewis Carroll might have composed.[70] And, as even Scott realizes, this poem as well as its "anger" is "much more controlled, and indeed contrived, than it looks."[71] Its initial query of whom to complain to may be seen as a literary formula and appears in much the same form at the beginning of another of Dunbar's poems, "Quhom to sall I compleine my wo" (no. 21).[72]

In this poem, after saying that he does not know who, among rich or poor, is his friend or his foe (3–4), the poet calls on his "Lord" for help: "Lord, how sall I my dayis dispone? / For lang service rewarde is none, / And schort my lyfe may heir indure" (6–8). Although this address may seem again to be to the king, the last stanza of the poem makes it clear that the poet is praying to God:

> Lord! sen in tyme sa sone to cum
> *De terra surrecturus sum,*
> Rewarde me with na erthlie cure,
> Bot me ressave *in regnum tuum.*
> Sen in this warld may non assure.
>
> (81–85)

Instead of working for worldly goods, which will not last, the poet would prefer a seat in heaven to an "erthlie cure."

Similarly, in "This waverand warldis wretchidnes" (no. 13)[73] after stating in detail "The failyeand and frutless bissines" (2), "the fals confort" of this life (6), and the fact that the world moves "fro weill to wo" (21), Dunbar points to his own condition of waiting for a benefice (53–88). At the end of this complaint, he asks for assistance:

> And for my curis in sindrie place,
> With help, Sir, of your nobill Grace,
> My sillie saule sall never be slane,
> Na for sic syn to suffer pane.
>
> (89–92)

Again, after stating that he is tiring of "this fals failyeand warld" (94), he writes in the last stanza:

> The formest hoip yit that I have
> In all this warld, sa God me save,
> Is in your Grace, bayth crop and grayne,
> Quhilk is ane lessing of my pane.
>
> (97–100)

The references here have been consistently taken as being to the king,[74] and, indeed, James IV would seem to be the likely candidate for bestower of the poet's wished-for benefice. But at the same time the poem is in the form of a rejection of this world and its unsure goods—made most meaningful by the example of the poet's long-awaited benefice. And in this sense it represents a turning from the world to the values beyond it. When Dunbar writes that with help his "sillie saule sall never be slane" (91), he is certainly alluding to the salvation that only God can give; and it is this Lord who should be considered as his "formest hoip" (97)—the expression "sa God me save" (98) being in this sense more than a line filler. Here at the least Dunbar seems to be intentionally associating king and God. How much in these poems is "for real," how much literary tradition, and how much standard moralizing is not clear. But what should be apparent is that these petitions can only be ambiguous when viewed as personal utterances.

IV   *The Touch of Whimsy*

In other poems within the genre of begging-poem, Dunbar's words to the king reveal obvious whimsy. In "Schir, for your Grace bayth nicht and day" (no. 18),[75] he repeats over and over, in the refrain to each of the eight stanzas, his wish that the king would be Joan Thomson's man, that is, in the proverbial Scots expression, someone who is ruled by his wife. If such were the caes, says the poet, he knows he would have his benefice. Part of the humor here lies in Dunbar's apparent irreverence, and part lies in the ridiculousness of the suggestion that it would be better if the ruler of the realm were not the head of his own household, especially when in the medieval view right rule began at hime, and in the Christian view the husband was properly ruler of his wife. Dunbar's "wish" in this poem is so outrageous that there could be no question of its being meant, or taken, seriously. He consciously plays the fool as he suggests that he would give all he had if the king would swear to be for a year Joan Thomson's man (17–20), and that in the future whenever he thinks that the king is being "harde or dour, / Or mercyles" in not helping him, he will pray to God and sweet Saint Anne that he were Joan Thomson's man (29–30).

Such outrageous foolery appears in another form in "I thocht lang quhill sum lord come hame" (no. 24),[76] when Dunbar views the lord treasurer of Scotland as existing in effect to take care of him—for him he is, as the refrain states, "my awin" lord treasurer. Because he feels that he will now receive his payment, he gives the treasurer a resounding welcome. His song would have been sad, he says, had he been forced to wait for his wage; now he can "sing with heart onsair" (23). Now he welcomes the lord treasurer as his own benefice, rent, livelihood, and pension (25–27).[77] It may not be clear whether the ironic tone of these poems is one of defensiveness, or whether the poet is using the device of the begging-poem to express his sense of ironic whimsy. Irony is, however, doubtless present; and in at least one instance it results in a first-rate poem.

In "Now lufferis cummis with larges lowd" (no. 22),[78] Dunbar's image of himself as an old horse who has run long in bare pasture and who is driven away from the stall by great court horses presents an effective blend of pathos and bitterness, sincerity and humor. The piece could easily have become a maudlin display of self pity, and, indeed, the high point of the pathos comes when the poet writes that his life has been so miserable that all he has to offer for sustenance is his flesh, but he hopes that after his death the king will not let the cobblers have his hide to gnaw (55–58). The court has made him a wornout mule; but, says the poet, if he were given new trappings to wear at Christmas, he would willingly be spurred at every limb.[79] The poem has a happy ending in the so-called "*Respontio Regis*," a final stanza which may very well be by Dunbar himself, in which the king is seen to order "this gray hors, Auld Dumbar," to be taken in and clothed at the king's expense.[80]

Despite any possible validity to the poet's charges of neglect— what Ridley calls "the glaring discrepancy between the poet's service and its reward"[81]—we should recognize that Dunbar is consciously and purposely overstating his claim, using hyperbole to take his audience beyond the realm of sympathy, drawing out the horse metaphor beyond the realm of seriousness. That is, the poem is a conscious study in pathos, which takes pity to the point of humor;[82] and, indeed, the poem is acceptable because we realize that its author is not really being maudlin or indulging in self-pity. It is his humorous overview that keeps the poem from being embarrassing and that actually allows us to view it as a piece of literature. The poet's meager request, which is clearly inappropriate to the condition described, helps provide this distancing. Dunbar may well be asking for additional apparel and subsistence, but he is hardly to be seen as a poor, old, ill beggar raising an agonized cry to the king. To see this poem revealing "the plight of old Dunbar in the winter of life turned loose to scrabble for a living,"[83] is to misread it and to misunderstand the ironic sense that marks Dunbar's poetry and view of life.

The old-age references and horse image appear together in another petition that may be compared to this one. Beginning, "Schir, yit remembir as of befoir, / How that my youthe is done forloir, / In your service, with pane and greiff " (no. 20),[84] it asks the king to recall and reward, as he did earlier, Dunbar's long service to him. Later in this eighty-five-line poem, the poet laments that when others flatter and feign, he can only "ballattis breif," write poems (47–48): "Sic barneheid leidis my brydill reynye" (49), that is, such childishness controls his bridle reins.[85] The image is once again that of Dunbar as horse, this time as one whose bridle reins are controlled by his simple art; unlike others he cannot plot and connive.

Whereas in "Now lufferis cummis," Dunbar sustained the horse image for the entire twelve stanzas of the poem, in "Schir, yit remembir" it is but one image of many; and, in fact, the poem presents a strange mixture of disparate images. For thirty lines bird images are developed. Dunbar compares himself to a red hawk who, now that its feathers have begun to molt, is not allowed to come to the lure (7–9), and to one of the "falcounis kynd," a "gentill goishalk," who goes unfed while lesser fowls are remembered and fed well (11–14). The contrasts emphasize the need for discerning that which is real. The magpie with the pretty coat may pretend to sing the song of the nightingale, but she is not able to reach the high note (16–17). In the common view birds farthest away are thought to have the fairest feathers; even though they cannot sing—"have no sang bot yowlis"—they are put in silver cages in the place of honor. In the world's view congenial native nests hatch only owls (21–24). The culmination of this bird imagery comes when Dunbar addresses the "gentile egill" and asks why he does not give relief to his subjects.

In the next part of the poem Dunbar shifts from bird to man and, moving from the "gentill" to the "sempill," says that after everyone is served—even the kin of "Rauf Colyard and Johine the Reif"—he still gets nothing (31–34), though he too comes "of Adame and Eve,/ And fane wald leif as utheris dois" (38–39). To avoid existing in such an unfavorable position, he would be a "pykthank," a flatterer, if such were not offensive to God (41–44). Rather than flatter he can "bot ballattis breif." Still he emphasizes that his petition to the king is an appeal to "mercye," not one based on "rycht" (52). At this point the dominant image of the poem changes once again as the poet requests "sum medecyne," specifically a benefice, to remedy his "maledie," that is, apparently, the "exces of thocht" that does "mischief" to him, as is reiterated seventeen times in the refrain of the poem (54–60). As if finally to prove his case, the poet says that in infancy, when he was on his nurse's knee, he was called "dandillie, bischop, dandillie" (61–62) a phrase that seems to combine a nursery term with the name of a clerical office. Now, in old age, complains Dunbar, "A sempill vicar I can not be" (64); undeserving and boorish tricksters get the dispensations he should have (66–75). He does not intend, he emphasizes, to reprove the king, though he is not far from doing so: "I say not, sir, yow to repreiff, / Bot doutles I go rycht neir hand it" (78–79). And he concludes the poem with still another image, a soul in purgatory living in pain but yet having hope of glory (81–82).

This poem is strange, even for Dunbar, and frequent differences in the readings of the Maitland and Bannatyne manuscripts do not help matters. One might well wonder about its unity and about Dunbar's control over his material. Is the personal element here so dominant that it gets in the way of the craftmanship; is Dunbar so blinded that he actually tells the king that he is on the verge of blaming him for not paying attention to the poet's needs?[86] Although the personal element may be more apparent than in other begging poems, it is still subordinate to the poetry. Dominant once again, from beginning to end, are outrageous overstatement and humorous metaphor. To blame Dunbar for not writing a poem having one main image pattern is not to give him his *donnée*.

The poem may profitably be seen as a demonstration of Dunbar's point that "barneheid leidis my brydill reynye" (49) and a proof of what he repeats over and over in the refrain, "Exces of thocht dois me mischeif." Like a child, a fool, or a madman, the poet raves; and while there may be truth in his complaint, the enjoyment lies in hearing the various excesses. "Exces of thocht" has produced excess of imagery and excess of boldness as he tells the king that he is nearly at the point of reproving him. Games are mentioned late in the poem, and while functioning to reprove falseness and cheating—Jok has "ane fals cairt in to his sleif " (68)—and to show the workings of fortune—Michell "playis with *totum* and I with *nychell*" (74)—they also reflect the element of play dominant in the conception of this poem. No matter how irreverent the poet may be, no matter how disruptive his jumps from one image to another, and no

matter how tedious his harpings on the subject of his promotion, all
is explained by his being a poet and suffering from "exces of thocht."
The ailment resembles that referred to in "My heid did yak yester
nicht," though here the humor is more apparent.

V   *The Proper Concerns*

A major reason for doubting the sincerity of Dunbar's many requests for benefice, clothing, and money is provided by several
other poems that speak against man's desire for earthly goods and
against the "covetice" that is the way of the world. As Dunbar wrote
at the conclusion of "Quhom to sall I compleine my wo," addressing
God, "Rewarde me with na erthlie cure, / Bot me ressave *in regnum
tuum*. / Sen in this warld may non assure" (83–85). He makes the
same point elsewhere (no. 67), addressing man:

> Man, pleis thy makar and be mirry,
> And sett not by this warld a chirry;
> Wirk for the place of paradyce,
> For thairin ringis na covettyce.[87]

Dunbar is doing more than paying lip service to the traditional
Christian teaching that "Welth, warldly gloir, and riche array" are
all but thorns laid in man's way.[88] Indeed, several of his better
poems are outspoken warnings against greed and homilies on the
right use of temporalia. A full presentation of this idea is found in
"Full oft I mus and hes in thocht" (no. 69),[89] having the refrain "For
to be blyth me think it best." Not only should man not care about
"this fals warld" or berate fortune for his condition, he should see
the world's goods in a proper perspective:

> Off wardlis gud and grit riches,
> Quhat fruct hes man but mirines?
> Thocht he this warld had eist and west,
> All wer povertie but [without] glaidnes;
> For to be blyth me thynk it best.

(21–25)

The need for human contentment is real. As Dunbar writes in the
first lines of the poem commonly cited as *Of Content* (no. 70),
"Quho thinkis that he hes sufficence, / Off gudis hes no indigence"
(1–2). Conversely, "quho in warld moist covatus is / In world is

purast man, I wis" (31–32). Another poem in this spirit—called by Scott "this rather forced mood of being happy with what you've got"[90]—begins, "Be mirry, man! and tak nocht far in mynd / The wavering of this wrechit warld of sorrow" (no. 73),[91] and has as its refrain "Without glaidness availis no tressour."

Concerning *Of Content* in particular, Scott calls it "A remarkable poem to come from this most discontented of poets: but again, he is doing a piece of conventional moralising."[92] Granted that this and the other "moralizing" poems are well within a medieval tradition, stemming from Boethius, and that to them may be joined hundreds of comparable pieces—notably Chaucer's ballade *Truth*—is it sufficient to dismiss them as conventional and to feel that the begging poems are where Dunbar is being unconventional, even personal, and that there he is "unburdening himself?"[93] We might well wonder about the relationship of these moralizing poems to the petitions where Dunbar repeatedly stresses his need for temporalia—for clothing, money, and benefice. The answer cannot be found by theorizing that the petitions represent one phase of Dunbar's life and thought, and the moralizings another phase. Notwithstanding the difficulties of dating Dunbar's poems, it is likely that most of them—including all of his petitions and moralizings—were written after 1503, and by that year Dunbar was an ordained priest.[94] Nor can the problem be solved by suggesting that Dunbar the court poet was essentially different from Dunbar the cleric, or that a poet does not have to live by the "moral truth" he expresses in his writing;[95] for in Dunbar's case the "moral truth" is expressed in both petitions and moralizings.

Although the problem is aggravated by our not knowing the precise chronology of these poems, it is more the result of our not recognizing that Dunbar's attitude toward earthly wealth is essentially ironic. In "Off every asking followis nocht" (no. 14), [96] Dunbar not only gives advice about the proper way of asking for "rewaird," but points out especially that overstatement is not effective (8–9), that "Few wordis may serve the wyis: / In asking sowld discretioun be" (24–25)—advice that would seem on the surface to be the opposite of his insistence in the petitions. He also concludes with a statement that puts reward in its proper place: although a lord will sometimes reward long service, "Gife [if] he dois not, quhat remedy? / To fecht [fight] with fortoun is no wit" (43–45). Moreover, this poem is properly seen as the first of three pieces on "dis-

cretioun"—the first on asking, the second on giving, and the third
on taking—all emphasizing in their refrains "discretioun," a term
meaning both discernment and moderation, especially in the Aris-
totelian sense.[97] The three poems together provide instruction in
making balanced judgments of value. In stating the responsibilities
of asker, giver, and taker, they function as essays on moral
philosophy.[98]

An additional poem that may help us to understand Dunbar's
petitions is "Sanct Salvatour! send silver sorrow" (no. 1).[99] Granting
the possible associations in this first line with St. Salvator's College
of St. Andrew's University and the need for alliteration, we may still
interpret the line as saying, in effect, "Holy Saviour! send sorrow to
silver."[100] Dunbar continues, saying with ironic humor that silver,
that is, money, "grevis me both evin and morrow, / Chasing fra me
all cheritie" (2–3). Silver deserves sorrow from heaven because it is
responsible for man's losing his feelings of Christian love. But no
one in the late Middle Ages—certainly not a cleric—could seriously
think to blame something in God's creation for man's misuse of it.
The humor is even more apparent in the image of the purse with its
associations with genitalia—in the refrain Dunbar writes "My
panefull purs so priclis me"—and in a later stanza he makes the
image even more vivid—"My purs is maid of sic ane skyn, / Thair
will na cors byd it within" (21–22). The "cors" or cross—a coin with
the cross on it—is ironically opposed to the purse: "Fra it as fra the
Feynd thay fle" (23). This image, in some ways like that of the horse
in "Now lufferis cummis with larges lowd," not only permeates the
poem, it creates a context for viewing Dunbar's point.

Although since Hailes' 1770 edition the poem has been titled *To
the King* and seen as addressed "to the King himself,"[101] the king's
role is more implied than stated. The reference to "My Lord" in the
last stanza (33) may be taken on one level as an address to James IV,
but it more immediately appears to be a restatement of the "Sanct
Salvatour" on whom the poet calls in the first line. The contrast
created in the poem is clearly between God—and charity—and the
Devil (referred to twice, 23, 29,)—and the "pricking." The poet
creates the premise that lack of worldly wealth is what causes his
purse to "prick" him. If, he theorizes, silver could always be in it
(28), then, apparently because of the cross on the coins, the Devil
would have no "dominatioun" over him (29). Even this point is
presented humorously, as Dunbar writes that if he could find a man

who could make on his purse "ane conjuratioun" (27)—that is, who could cast spells on it so as to cause silver to be always in it—the Devil would then have no power over him. The humor is, of course, first, that if a spell were cast on him he would be in the Devil's power; and, second, that the Devil is traditionally associated with money. According to St. Francis, for instance—whom Dunbar cites elsewhere—it was better for man to handle excrement than to touch money.

The last stanza of the poem should be read in this context:

> I haif inquyrit in mony a place,
> For help and confort in this cace,
> And all men sayis, My Lord, that ye
> Can best remeid for this malice [disease],
> That with sic panis prickillis me.
>
> (31–35)

The king can certainly help by giving him silver, but it is Christ who can help free him from worldly desires. The motifs of the begging poem and Christian moralizing would seem to come together here. It is difficult to see the validity of Scott's analysis that the piece "is remarkable for its sincerely-felt, finely-expressed presentation of the case against poverty."[102] To think that when Dunbar complains that thoughts of poverty ("pansing of penuritie") rob him of thoughts of pleasant diversions ("plesand pastance") like singing and dancing (11–14), he means what he is saying, is to fail to appreciate the poet's medieval Christian heritage or his own sense of ironic humor. The poem is a begging poem on only one level; on another, and more important, level it is a tongue-in-cheek juxtaposition of human pleasures and the ideals of Dunbar's religion. As such it may act as a key for our understanding the other petitions, where Dunbar uses a traditional form for his own purposes—and these are entirely in accord with his Christian beliefs.

Notwithstanding what is revealed in most of the petitions, Dunbar's real attitude toward the king may be found in *A New Year's Gift to the King* (no. 26),[103] which may be quoted in its entirety:

> My prince in God, gif the guid grace,
> Joy, glaidnes, confort, and solace,
> Play, pleasance, myrth, and mirrie cheir,
>   In hansill [first gift] of this guid new yeir.

5   God gif to the ane blissed chance,
     And of all vertew aboundance,
     And grace ay for to perseveir,
         In hansill of this guid new yeir.

     God give the guid prosperitie,
10   Fair fortoun and felicitie,
     Evir mair in earth quhill thow ar heir,
         In hansell of this guid new yeir.

     The heavinlie Lord his help the send,
     Thy realme to reull and to defend,
15   In peace and justice it to steir,
         In hansell of this guid new yeir.

     God gif the blis quharevir thow bownes [go],
     And send the many Fraunce crownes,
     Hie liberall heart and handis not sweir [disinclined (to give)],
20   In hansell of this guid new yeir.

Even with the possible hint in the last stanza that the king should be
liberal in his own giving, this piece is far from being a begging poem
at all and far from containing any sort of reproach of James. It has
been explained as an early poem, "written before Dunbar desired a
benefice,"[104] and dismissed as "a graceful, light, occasional piece
reflecting a custom that went back to the days of the Roman Em-
pire."[105]

Moving from his wish that the king will have happiness, the poet
prays that God will give him abundance of virtue and "guid pros-
peritie," and that with the help of "the heavenlie Lord," the king
will rule his realm in peace and justice. The ideals stated here are
precisely those to be found in the moralizings and demonstrate what
true charity is. Rather than ask anything of the king, the poet-cleric
is in his own way giving to the king a first gift ("hansill") that should
be the basis of all gifts. Avoiding any pose here—of petitioner,
critic, or fool—Dunbar affirms his belief in his "prince in God,"
stating at the same time the necessary and proper relationship between earthly and heavenly rule. But the gifts offered are not really
Dunbar's; they are the gifts of the Holy Spirit, and the poet is, in
effect, praying that the king can receive them and use them well.

No matter what else may be said about Dunbar's life in court and
relationship to king and queen, this poem reveals an essential side of
it, one that is perhaps at the bottom of all the foolery and play. No

matter how Dunbar the character figures in these poems, he must always be seen as subordinate to, and as a creation of, Dunbar the poet. Whatever comedy and irony may appear elsewhere, the poem "My prince in God" exists as a straightforward statement that reveals better than other poems the essential "condicioun" of this "makar."

CHAPTER 3

The Court Poet

I *Panegyrics*

THE world of most of Dunbar's poetry is the court of James IV at Edinburgh. James's reign, from 1488 to 1513, encompassed Dunbar's poetic career so exactly that in one sense it is only fitting for the court—including king, queen, courtiers, and ladies-in-waiting—to provide the great bulk of the particulars in his writing. Places and characters come from the court—as in the *Dance in the Quenis Chalmer*. Its special events—such as the marriage of James and Margaret Tudor—provided occasions and settings for his poems. But, even more significantly, Dunbar's view of the world was from the vantage point of the court; it influenced his vision and his perspective. He saw feast days like Christmas and New Year's from its point of view, and he looked at the world outside the court through its critical eyes.

Just as James's temperament dominated the court and determined, for good and bad, the fortunes of Scotland, so it is likely to have influenced Dunbar and the nature of his poetry. On the one hand, the king was well educated, apparently fluent in Latin, Spanish, French, Gaelic, German, Flemish, and Italian, and very much interested in science and medicine. He was also strangely religious: he supposedly would not ride on Sunday, even to Mass, and he apparently wore an iron belt under his garb as penance for his role in the death of his father. He was also fascinated with the chivalric, not only holding tournaments but trying, in effect, to make Edinburgh another Camelot. On the other hand, James was bawdy, irreverent, a practical joker, headstrong, and noted for his amorous escapades.[1] Although the blend of these opposites was unique in James, a comparable blend of the reverent and the bawdy, the intellectual and the physical, the sober and the irreverent, marks the writings of Dunbar, who has been thought of as James's poet laureate.

Although in his poetry Dunbar frequently played the fool for the king with his invective and his laughter, he was participating in a long tradition that recognized the interconnection of wisdom and folly, as well as of poetry and folly. Renaissance drama is full of wise fools—most notably Mad Tom and the Fool in *King Lear*; and the Clown in *Twelfth Night*, who is said to be "wise enough to play the fool, / and to do that well, craves a kind of wit."[2] Writers of the period celebrated the interrelationship of wisdom and folly—notably Erasmus in his *Praise of Folly*—and various jest books contained anecdotes of wise fools. Many medieval and Renaissance courts contained notable fools—such as Ciaiesius at the court of Grand Duke Ferdinand I of Florence who was a gifted exponent of law and philosophy as well as a fool, and who later went to the University of Pisa to obtain an advanced degree. Closer to Scotland and to Dunbar's time was John Skelton, who was a poet laureate at the court of Henry VIII in London, a cleric, and a notable fool.

At the same time, Dunbar functioned as something of an official panegyrist, who would praise and celebrate for the king and the court. It was doubtless in something of this capacity that Dunbar welcomed Bernard Stewart, lord of Aubigny, a great Scots general who had fought for the French, when he returned to Scotland in May, 1508.[3] Although too full of hyperbole to appeal to modern tastes,[4] the poem welcoming Stewart (no. 61) is necessarily in the high style appropriate to stately occasions:

> Welcum, in were [war] the secund Julius,
> The prince of knightheyd, and flour of chevalry;
> Welcum, most valyeant and victorius;
> Welcum, invincible victour moste wourthy;
> Welcum, our Scottis chiftane most dughti;
> Wyth sowne of clarioun, organe, song, and sence,
> To the atonis [at once], Lord, Welcum all we cry;
> With glorie and honour, lawde and reverence.
>
> (17–24)

While using commonplaces of praise, Dunbar is still able to make the language of his poetry participate in the celebration and suggest the great joy and pride felt by the Scottish people. As a celebratory piece this poem may be seen as a straightforward example of the kind of writing parodied by Dunbar in his *Welcome to the Lord Treasurer* (no. 24). It is doubtless in this same quasi-official capacity that Dunbar lamented the death of Bernard Stewart a month later (no. 62).[5] The language may again strike our ears as excessive,[6] but, acting as a companion piece to the previous celebratory poem, this elegy shows Dunbar's mastery of rhetorical traditions associated with the elegiac, as well as his ability to alter the tone of his verses so as to convey his sadness and sense of loss:

> O duilfull death! O dragon dolorous!
>   Quhy hes thow done so dulfullie devoir
> The prince of knychtheid, nobill and chevilrous,
>   The witt of weiris, of armes and honour,
> The crop of curage, the strenth of armes in stour [battle],
> The fame of France, the fame of Lumbardy,
>   The chois of chiftanes, most awfull in airmour,
> The charbuckell, cheif of every chevelrie!

                                                                    (17–24)

Dunbar's paramount effort as a court panegyrist is the so-called *Thrissil and the Rois* (no. 55),[7] an epithalamion in honor of the marriage of James and Margaret in 1503. Written in rhyme royal, the stanzaic form first used in English by Chaucer that became the vehicle in the fifteenth and sixteenth centuries for almost all overtly serious poetry, it contains the major conventions of medieval courtly narrative: it is allegorical, a dream vision, and about love. The narrator is told to rise from his bed and honor May. In a garden he sees Nature who crowns the lion king of beasts, the eagle king of birds, and the thistle king of flowers. To the thistle Nature entrusts the rose, seen here as red and white and as the most perfect of flowers. After flowers and birds praise the rose, the narrator awakens and the poem ends. Very much in the manner of Chaucer's *Parliament of Fowls* and perhaps influenced by the aureate diction of the French *Grands Rhétoriqueurs*—that is, polysyllabic coinages from Latin— and heraldic symbolism, it is even more excessive in its use of artifice than the Bernard Stewart poem. One might wish to think that in this and such poems Dunbar was only following orders and producing something on command; but in his canon are two other notable allegories, *Bewty and the Presoneir* and the *Goldyn Targe* (nos. 54, 56), that likewise reveal aureate diction. As C. S. Lewis has written of aureate terms, "They are in language what the gorgeous armours of tournament were in life; the proper expression for a vision of brightness, largesse, ceremony, exhilaration."[8] And whereas our age may not especially enjoy the high style that uses them, we might recognize that they were a way of poetic ex-

perimentation, a means of allowing the vernacular to participate in
the high style and to equal the languages of Antiquity.

In the *Thrissil and the Rois*, called by Schipper the "finest of all
Dunbar's allegorical poems"[9] and by Lewis "a triumph of fruitful
obedience to conventions" and a "minuet of conventions,"[10] Dunbar
is hardly weighed down or imprisoned by the high style and its
conventions of allegory, structure, and language. When he presents
May awakening his narrator and commanding him to write something in her honor, he has the narrator argue with May:

> "Quhairto," quod I, "sall I uprys at morrow,
> For in this May few birdis herd I sing?
> Thai haif moir caus to weip and plane thair sorrow,
> Thy air it is nocht holsum nor benyng;
> Lord Eolus dois in thy sessone ring;
> So busteous ar the blastis of his horne,
> Amang thy bewis to walk I haif forborne [refrained]."
>
> (29–35)

The voice is that of reason speaking out in a world of the unreal, but
it is present not for the purpose of criticizing the conventions of
allegory. Rather, this voice from the waking world, one that knows
what a Scottish spring is really like, clearly does not belong in the
poem. It is the voice of the low or plain style, in the midst of the
high style, the literalist in the realm of the symbolic; and the result
of its intrusion is comic relief.

In response to this literal view of the seasons, May "sobirly did
smyll" (36) and tells him to do as he had promised, to describe "the
Ros of most plesance" (39) and to go see how the birds sing and
dance. Still apparently not believing, the narrator dresses himself in
shirt and coat ("serk and mantill," 46) and follows her into a garden,
whose description immediately contrasts with the familiar waking
world the poet had been invoking to May: "The purpour sone, with
tendir bemys reid, / In orient bricht as angell did appeir, / Throw
goldin skyis putting up his heid" (50–52). It is such color, such rich
language, here perhaps especially noticeable and effective because
of the juxtaposition with the narrator's plain speech, that a poem like
this allows to come into being. The imminent marriage of James and
Margaret, far from acting to contain or stifle the poet's art, represents a stage on which it might be exhibited, an occasion for a kind of
writing not possible in the ordinary world with its ordinary events.

The richness is not only found in the adjectives or the imagery; it is created by the references to mythology—"Dame Nature gaif ane inhibitioun thair / To fers Neptunus, and Eolus the bawld, / Nocht to perturb the wattir nor the air" (64–66)—by cataloging and anaphora (repetition of terms)—"Haill May, haill Flora, haill Aurora schene, / Haill princes Natur, haill Venus luvis quene" (62–63)— and by heraldic symbolism like that presenting James in three symbolic forms. He is the lion (87), emblem of royal mercy and of the royal arms of Scotland; the eagle (120), emblem of royal liberality; and the thistle (129), heraldic emblem of Scotland. If Dunbar were painting a picture, he could have all three emblems existing at the same time; in his word picture he must present them diachronically. But his treatment allows for an emphasis not easily created in a picture. The three emblems repeating the signification emphasize the king's majesty, especially his justice and mercy. It might have been difficult to find comparable animals and birds to represent Margaret's qualities, but in the rose—"the fresche Ros of cullour reid and quhyt" (142)—Dunbar had a ready-made symbol, one already having heraldic associations with England—Margaret was daughter of Elizabeth of York, whose emblem was the white rose, and Henry, whose house of Lancaster was represented by the red rose. The rose also had allegorical associations with love—not only through the *Roman de la Rose*, but through the Song of Songs and the various hymns to the Virgin Mary—and even with marriage—as was seen in the interlaced rose and thistle already marking the new windows of Holyrood Palace, and the intertwined roses and thistles, along with daisies,[11] in the marriage contract between James and Margaret. Dunbar affirms that no other flower—not even the lily (150), emblem of France—is so perfect as the rose. The poem ends with a song praising the rose and welcoming her in language that expresses the virtues suggested by this flower, and wishing that Christ will keep her from all adversity (182). The *Thrissil and the Rois* is finally like Dunbar's *New Year's Gift to the King* (no. 26). It is his gift to James and Margaret on the occasion of their marriage; not only a poem honoring them, it is a work of art that they have inspired and that is theirs.

It is likewise as a court poet that Dunbar looks at the realm around him. He criticizes the burghers of Edinburgh for not sufficiently valuing their city, home of the king's court and the law court, to keep it clean (no. 44).[12] He warns that if the courts go to another city, Edinburgh will lose its great name. And, on the other

hand, he praises Aberdeen for its reception of Queen Margaret in
1511 (no. 64):

> Blyth Aberdeane, thow beriall of all tounis,
>   The lamp of bewtie, bountie, and blythnes;
> Unto the heaven ascendit thy renoun is
>   Off vertew, wisdome, and of worthines;
>   He [high] nottit is thy name of nobilnes,
> Into the cuming of oure lustie Quein,
>   The wall of welth, guid cheir, and mirrines:
> Be blyth and blisfull, burgh of Aberdein.[13]

Again epideictic rhetoric fills the poem, but even though Dunbar is
obviously indulging in hyperbole, his celebration of the city and
memorialization of its gracious reception act implicitly as a celebration of the Scottish people and of their queen.

II   *Play and Entertainment*

With the freedom of court poet Dunbar was able to look around
the court and laugh at what he saw, at both the people and the
manners. Although he names some courtiers and ladies-in-waiting
by name—for instance, Sir John Sinclair, Master Robert Scha, Mistress Musgrave in the *Dance in the Quenis Chalmer* (no. 32)—he is
by and large interested in them less as people than as names, especially names he can play with. James Dog, keeper of the queen's
wardrobe, not only provides a stanza of canine imagery in this poem
(43–49), he also appears as the subject of two other poems, one "The
Wardraipper of Venus boure" (no. 33) in which for six stanzas Dunbar again plays with dog terms. The work culminates with Dunbar's
playfully warning the queen that this Dog is too great to be her lap
dog—his walking even causes the rooms to shake—and closes with
the refrain, "Madam, ye heff a dangerous Dog!" (21–24). Providing
a mate to this poem is "O gracious Princes, guid and fair" (no. 34), in
which Dunbar apparently reverses himself and praises Dog, in his
refrain playing again with the name: "He is na Dog; he is a Lam."
The humor of the juxtaposed animal images is furthered by the
context provided by the previous "Dog" poem.

It would be wrongheaded to see these poems as being against
James Dog. He has merely provided the name and thus functions as

equivalent to the occasions of the celebrations. These poems are good-humored plays of language; they are like the celebratory poems in providing an opportunity for the poet, but different from them in being essentially comic. Both pieces—and probably the *Dance in the Quenis Chalmer*—are apparently directed to Queen Margaret and probably designed to provide amusement for this young girl—she was thirteen when she married James. In them Dunbar again plays the fool, but here he plays with language and with people as linguistic entities, as grist for the mill of poetry.

The high point of Dunbar's mock verse is probably "Now lythis off ane gentill knycht" (no. 35). Apparently modeled on Chaucer's *Tale of Sir Thopas*, which has the same substance and verse form,[14] the poem ostensibly praises a man—Sir Thomas Norny, as he is called —who was really a court fool, though whether by profession or by nature is not clear. Still, knowing who Norny really was is of little importance to the poem or to our appreciating its humor, which centers on the incongruous blending of the chivalric and the homely:

> Now lythis [listen] off ane gentill knycht,
> Schir Thomas Norny, wys and wycht [strong],
>   And full of chevelry;
> Quhais father was ane giand keyne [bold],
> His mother was ane Farie Queyne,
>   Gottin be sossery.
>
>   (1–6)

And so it goes for fifty-four lines. Although lacking the scope and development of Chaucer's *Thopas* or the scores of allusions to medieval romance found in this earlier poem, Dunbar's piece is a far more unified composition than Chaucer's ostensibly incomplete effort. It is also possible that Dunbar may have been relying on his audience's familiarity with Chaucer's poem and on their seeing relationships between Sir Thomas and Sir Thopas. Chaucer's work would then provide a context for Dunbar's, a given that the Scots poet could partake of, thereby keeping his composition short.

Dunbar's playfulness culminates in his reference to Norny as "Lord of evere full [every fool], / That in this regeone duellis," and in his assertion that this "hy renowned knycht . . . wanttis no thing bot bellis" (50–54). The allusion is at once to the bells customarily associated with knights' horses and to those also customarily associated with fools and jesters. Dunbar's method here is rather like Chaucer's in the General Prologue to the *Canterbury Tales* when he compares the jingling bells on the Monk's bridle to the chapel bell, thus linking the knight *manqué* and the lapsed contemplative. The humor in Dunbar's poem would be even greater if Norny were really neither knight nor fool;[15] in presenting him as the former Dunbar is really making him the latter, and the two states come together, as it were, in the image of the bells.

Although "Now lythis off ane gentill knycht" is, unlike the Dog poems, a satiric portrayal of its subject, Norny, it may be even more an oblique criticism of chivalry, at least as it existed at James's court. As such "Now lythis" may join Dunbar's comic account of a tournament between a shoemaker and a tailor (no. 58), where the satire is more apparent. Whereas Norny is compared to several traditional heroes, only one of these is unambiguously a knight—"Sir Bevis the knycht off Southe Hamptowne" (35), also mentioned in *Sir Thopas*. But although literally the son of a nobleman, Bevis is not notably chivalric, at least not in the Middle English romance bearing his name. As a boy he is sold as a slave and then exists for seven years as a prisoner, sitting in a dungeon using a stick to protect himself from dragons.

The other points of comparison in Dunbar's poem are mainly figures from the outlaw ballads:

> Was never wyld Robein under bewch,
> Nor yet Roger off Clekniskleuch,
>   So bauld a berne [man] as he;
> Gy off Gysburne, na Allan Bell,
> Na Simonis sonnes off Quhynfell,
>   At schot war never so slie.
>
> (25–30)

Whereas Robin and Guy of Gisborne are probably from the Robin Hood ballads, especially *Robin Hood and Guy of Gisborne*—Guy being a knight defeated by Robin—the other appellations are most likely variations of names found in *Adam Bell, Clym of the Clough, and William of Cloudesly*, another outlaw ballad; and "Simon's sons of Whinfell" would seem to be the family of freebooters mentioned in the Middle Scots poem *Cockelbie's Sow*. While part of the humor lies in the comparison of the knight Sir Thomas to these uncourtly heroes, part also lies in the presentation of these simple folk in relation to a knight. Although Norny himself may have been a particular target for Dunbar's insults, he is hardly essential to the poem or to its ironic humor. Rather than be inextricably bound to the court, this poem—like most of Dunbar's poems—uses the court as a jumping off point.

Related to these poems as court entertainment is *The Flyting of Dunbar and Kennedie* (no. 6), which should be viewed as one of Dunbar's major efforts as a court poet. Strange as it may appear to us today, the poem is well within a tradition stemming from classical antiquity, perhaps related to the Provençal *tenso* and *sirventes,* the French *jeu parti* and *débat,* as well as in native tradition to various Celtic contests of invective, in Old English to the words between Unferth and Beowulf in *Beowulf,* and in Middle English to the *Owl and the Nightingale.*[16] But to affirm the literary affinities of this poem is to do little with it; and indeed, except to furnish antecedents and analogues and to take literally the details brought up and see them as informative of Dunbar, few critics have known what to do with the work. Scott's evaluation of it as "the most repellent poem known to me in any language"[17] would, to one degree or another, probably be that of most modern readers.

Even while Scott recognizes that the *Flyting* "has many poetic merits and is a *tour-de-force* of language and versification," he feels "it must be condemned as a whole, being to poetry much what slander is to life"; and his criticism may be summed up in his evaluation of it as "an anti-poem."[18] Without going so far as Scott, Mackay writes that the *Flyting* "will always be one of the curiosities of literature," and adds that it has "the dubious honour of being the best representative of a bad style of poem which no one can wish to see revived."[19] Notwithstanding such criticism, the poem was very popular in the sixteenth century: not only was it published in the Chepman and Myllar printing, it was apparently the source of several imitations.[20] And if actually the account—or result—of a contest of invective, it was nevertheless regarded by contemporaries as more than a study in jangling, even as something worth memorializing.

The contest, insofar as it exists within the poem, is hardly for real. No matter what it purports to be, the poem is certainly not a serious attack on, or satire of, Kennedy, a fellow poet referred to fondly in "I that in heill wes and gladnes" (89); and the description of it in the Bannatyne manuscript as "iocuond and mirrie"[21] is clearly to the

point. The style of the two contestants, moreover, is so similar that
the whole composition might well be the work of a single author,
probably Dunbar.[22] It is not misleading, and may even be instruc-
tive, to view this poem, the longest in the Dunbar corpus, not as the
record of a contest but as the product of a single writer creating two
voices. That Dunbar was capable of handling such voices may be
seen in such poems as "This nycht in my sleip I wes agast" (no. 42)
and *The Tua Mariit Wemen and the Wedo* (no. 47). At the same
time, the *Flyting* differs from other contests found in Dunbar's
verse, such as that between the shoemaker and the tailor (no. 58),
for here there is no winner and no real frame stating the contest.

The poem begins *in medias res* with a challenge from Dunbar to
Kennedy, or, more precisely, with an address by Dunbar to his
second in the projected duel, Sir John the Ros, stating his complaint
against Kennedy and his second, Quentin, who have in their pride
placed themselves above the stars and who may share the fate of
Lucifer. If these poets should speak against him "in speciall," affirms
Dunbar, all of creation would feel his rage:

> The erd sould trymbill, the firmament sould schaik,
>   And all the air in vennaum suddane stink,
> And all the divillis of hell for redour [fear] quaik,
>   To heir quhat I sould wryt with pen and ynk;
>   For and I flyt, sum sege [man] for schame sould sink,
> The se sould birn, the mone sould thoill [suffer] ecclippis,
> Rochis sould ryfe [burst], the warld sould hald no grippis,
>   Sa loud of cair the commoun bell sould clynk.
>
>   (9–16)

And such is the hyperbole and exaggeration that follows. Even
though Dunbar is "wondir laith" to write this way—"Flyting to use
richt gritly I escham [am ashamed]; / For it is nowthir wynning nor
rewaird" (18–19)—he will, since such language is necessary. The
situation may be likened to that in the so-called *Complaint aganis
Mure* (no. 5), when Dunbar projects a situation that is a premise for
his subsequent play of language.

This introduction, occupying three stanzas, is followed by an answer by Kennedy, also in three stanzas. Then in twenty-five stanzas,
Dunbar hurls invective at his foe, followed in turn by thirty-eight
stanzas in which Kennedy replies in kind; and then the poem
ends.[23] Whereas in Chepman and Myllar the colophon at the end

addressing the audience reads, "Iudge 3e now heir quha gat the
war"—that is, who got the worse[24]—the structure of the poem is
such that Dunbar receives more criticism than Kennedy. Quantita-
tively at least, it would seem that Dunbar gets the worse, a judgment reinforced by Kennedy's having the final word. If such were
the case, the condemnation of Dunbar—especially if the whole
flyting were written by the poet himself—may well seem comparable to Chaucer's criticism of himself and his works in the dream
visions, notably in the Prologue to the *Legend of Good Women,* in
the Introduction to the *Man of Law's Tale,* and most directly in the
words of the Host after the *Tale of Sir Thopas,* when not only does
Chaucer apparently fail to win the tale-telling contest, he is actually
stopped in the middle of his effort. For the court audience, especially if the *Flyting* were designed for performance as an entertainment, additional humor would come from a situation where their
court poet, Dunbar, loses the duel he initiates.

But whatever any other purpose or point of the *Flyting,* it exists as
a study in language without rival in the English—including the
Middle Scots—language. Not only are the insults most likely the
particular products of the poet's fertile imagination, so are the
phrases used to convey them. The last two stanzas of Dunbar's
attack on Kennedy may be sufficient to demonstrate both the nature
of the invective and the extent of Dunbar's playing with language:

> Loun lyk Mahoun, be boun me till obey,
>   Theif, or in greif mischeif sall the betyd;
> Cry grace, tykis face, or I the chece and sle;
>   Oule, rare and yowle, I sall defowll thy pryd;
>   Peilet gled, baith fed and bred of bichis syd,
> And lyk ane tyk, purspyk, quhat man settis by the!
>   Forflittin, countbittin, beschittin, barkit hyd,
> Clym ledder, fyle tedder, foule edder, I defy the.
>
> Maunch muttoun, byt buttoun, peilit gluttoun, air to Hilhous;
>   Rank beggar, ostir dregar, foule fleggar in the flet;
> Chittirlilling, ruch rilling, lik schilling in the milhous;
>   Baird rehator, theif of natour, fals tratour, feyindis gett;
>   Filling of tauch, rak sauch, cry crauch, thow art our sett;
> Muttoun dryver, girnall ryver, yadswyvar, fowll fell the:
>   Herretyk, lunatyk, purspyk, carlingis pet,
> Rottin crok, dirtin dok, cry cok, or I sall quell the.
>
>   (233–48)[25]

While representative of the other stanzas in the poem, these tend more to subordinate sense to sound. That is, other stanzas are full of insults having an immediate meaning, most of the time a meaning that would seem especially significant to a court audience. But here the invective reaches a high point of dissonance. More dominant than sense are the patterns of assonance, consonance, and alliteration; and these suggest that they are what were of major interest not only to Dunbar but also to his audience, especially to an audience listening to a performance of this poem. Whereas most of Dunbar's writings profit from being read aloud, the *Flyting* demands such a reading.

Dunbar's humor—especially his irony and his caricature—may at times strike us as insensitive and cruel, not only in the *Flyting* but especially in the piece commonly called *Of ane Blak-Moir* (no. 37). As indicated by its last two stanzas, the poem may be alluding to "one of the most brilliant tournaments of the reign," one presided over by a black lady.[26] The tournament, first held in 1507, was apparently a great success and was repeated the next year. It suggests the kind of joking common during James's reign, and Dunbar may be reflecting, if not echoing, the king's joke when he calls for the losers of the tournament to be required to go behind this lady and "kis hir hippis" (23). But at the same time the poem may join the Norny piece in being an ironic comment on the chivalry of the time.

The first three stanzas of the poem, however, show what is probably Dunbar's main interest. In stanza 1, he says that having written about white ladies, he will now write of a black one who has recently arrived in the land. He wishes, he emphasizes, to describe her perfectly, this "ladye with the mekle lippis" (1–4); and he thus presents in the next two stanzas a vivid description:

> Quhou schou is tute mowitt lyk ane aep,
> And lyk a gangarall onto gaep;
>   And quhou hir schort catt nois up skippis;
> And quhou scho schynes lyk ony saep;
>   My ladye with the mekle lippis.
>
> Quhen schou is claid in reche apparrall,
> Schou blinkis als brycht as ane tar barrell;
>   Quhen schou was born, the son tholit clippis,
> The nycht be fain faucht in hir querrell:
>   My ladye with the mekle lippis.

$$(6–15)^{27}$$

While the language here resembles the invective of the *Flyting*, it is also like the descriptions found in Shakespeare's Dark Lady sonnets, especially in "In the old age black was not counted fair" and "My mistress's eyes are nothing like the sun."[28] In an age when black was traditionally seen as foul and the black man as monstrous and evil, even demonic, Dunbar could use convention in relation to the particular subject that provided the efficient cause of his poem.[29]

We should no more think that Dunbar was a racist in the modern sense of the word than we should think that his mockery of Norny showed him to be "against" fools, or that the insults in the *Flyting* revealed him to be "against" dwarfs. In fact, this poem is more like the Dog poems, with their play on James Dog's name, than it is like the Norny satire. Far from mocking the black woman, Dunbar plays with her unusual features—unusual to an early sixteenth-century Scotsman—as he played with Dog's likewise unusual name. According to the medieval idea of beauty, one's outward appearance was a reflection of one's internal nature, seen mainly through the face, specifically through the eyes and lips—as Dante emphasizes in describing Beatrice. The "blak" lady here with her "mekle lippis" would have seemed a grotesquerie to Dunbar's contemporaries, a living equivalent of the gargoyles common in medieval art, a parody of man comparable to ape, giant, and dwarf, and a perversion of nature sufficient, as the poem playfully presents it, to eclipse the sun (13). And the knights who will fight in the tournament that she presides over are like the "nycht" that fought on her behalf against the sun (14). To present this lady as the prize of a tournament is not so much to speak against her as to criticize tournaments. The negative reward of the winners—they do not have to "kis hir hippis"—is a further comment on the vacuousness of this courtly activity.

In all these poems Dunbar has been describing his subject from the point of view of the outside observer. In another, "I, Maister Andro Kennedy" (no. 40), the subject addresses us, delivering a lengthy monologue in lines of alternating Scots and Latin. Purporting to be the last will and testament of Andrew Kennedy—probably not the poet Kennedy of the *Flyting* but a "drunken court physician, now forgotten"[30]—the poem is a study in blasphemy made even more ironic by its use of Latin, the language of the religion that the speaker is rejecting, and by its echo of Psalms and the Office of the

Dead. Kennedy asserts that he has no belief, that he leaves his soul
to the wine cellar and his body to the dunghill:

> Nunc condo testamentum meum,
>   I leiff my saull for evermare,
> Per omnipotentem Deum,
>   In to my lordis wyne cellar;
> Semper ibi ad remanendum,
>   Quhill domisday without dissever.
> Bonum vinum ad bibendum,
>   With sueit Cuthbert that luffit me nevir.
>
> (17–24)[31]

Blasphemous as this might seem, the whole monologue is grounded
in fantasy, as the initial stanza makes clear when Kennedy says that
he was begotten by an incubus (3). With its mixing of languages and
confusion of secular and religious, it is also a grotesquerie, a play of
language on a par with the *Flyting*. Such testaments, moreover,
were common in the late Middle Ages and may even be thought of
as representing a verse genre. Best known of these poems is probably François Villon's *Grand Testament,* though in English Henryson, Skelton, and Lindsay wrote notable testaments.[32] Hardly to be
taken at face value, they are studies in folly, and indeed Kennedy
here assigns his folly to "Iok Fule," saying "In faith I am mair fule
than he" (73–75).[33]

III   *Satire and Criticism*

Although it is unlikely that such poems as the *Flyting* and "I,
Maister Andro Kennedy" are to be taken seriously, we might wonder whether they are essentially mocking and derisive or whether
they are mainly humorous plays of language, providing at once an
entertainment for king and court and a vehicle for Dunbar's poetic
artistry. There are, however, a few poems in which Dunbar seems
clearly to be "against" someone, in which his scorn is uncontestably
real. In the so-called *Epetaphe for Donald Owre* (no. 36), the poet
speaks against a public figure he regards as a vicious traitor and a
dangerous enemy of the realm. The occasion of the poem would
seem to be Donald's imprisonment in 1507, after he had launched
an unsuccessful revolt against James. Dunbar's point in writing this
mock epitaph is not to laugh at Donald Owre but most likely to

persuade the king that imprisonment is not enough, that he should be put to death.[34] As the last stanza states it, "The murtherer ay murthour mais, / And evir quhill he be slane he slais" (43–44), that is, the murderer will continue to murder until he is himself slain. Not only do the plain speech and short lines of this poem contrast with the formality and grandeur of a celebratory poem like that welcoming Bernard Stewart (no. 61), Dunbar's tone here is not one of humor. Even though the piece may be a mock epitaph, Dunbar is being deadly serious in what he says about Donald, as the first line suggests—"In vice most vicius he excellis." His statement of the man's insidiousness is quite different from the hyperbole and name-calling found in other poems.

To this epitaph may be compared two other poems in which Dunbar attacks John Damian, an Italian alchemist who had convinced James IV to support his quasi-scientific inquiries, especially those aimed at turning base metals into gold. Damian, who is made abbot of Tungland by James—doubtless to Dunbar's annoyance—is referred to several times in the treasurer's accounts from 1501 to 1513 as receiving money from the king, even as playing dice and cards with him.[35] In September, 1507, Damian tried to fly from Stirling Castle to France, promising to be there before the Scottish ambassadors who departed on the same date. As a result of this attempted flight Damian fell and broke his thigh, and thus provided Dunbar with material for two burlesque dream visions: "As yung Awrora, with cristall haile" (no. 38) and "Lucina schynnyng in silence of the nicht" (no. 39).[36] Dunbar's contempt for this foreigner he regarded as imposter, charlatan, and, doubtless, as usurper of a benefice that more legitimately should have been his, is pronounced; his scorn is savage; and his delight in Damian's fall obvious. As Damian appears in these two poems, he is falsehood personified and, even more, falsehood at its most ludicrous.[37] Still, Dunbar's attitude toward him is different from that toward Donald Owre, and the poems against the two men are more unalike than alike.

In the two Damian poems Dunbar plays with rhetorical and poetic convention. Both begin with aureate diction, dream visions, and the machinery of allegory; but juxtaposed against the high style are plain speech and satiric humor. In "As yung Awrora," for instance, Dunbar sets out in full dress: "As yung Awrora, with cristall haile, /In orient schew hir visage paile, /A swevyng [dream] swyth [quickly] did me assaile" (1–3). But soon contrasted with this elegance is the description of Damian's medical activities:

> He cowth gif cure for laxatyve,
> To gar [cause] a wicht [strong] hors want [lose] his lyve,
> Quha evir assay wald, man or wyve,
>   Thair hippis yeid [went] hiddy giddy.
>
>   (41–44)

The picture and the humor resemble what is found in the *Dance in the Quenis Chalmer*. Dunbar also alters the conventions of courtly poetry. The birds for instance, common in dream visions— such as the *Thrissil and the Rois*—for their songs and participation in love, appear here as defenders of the natural order. They battle the unnatural creature trying to fly, and attack him until he falls. As the poem describes their anger and hostility, the sound changes from the harmonious and elegant to the raucous, producing a holocaust of cacophony:

> The air was dirkit with the fowlis,
> That come with yawmeris and with yowlis,
> With skryking, skrymming, and with scowlis,
>   To tak him in the tyde.
>
>   (121–24)

The "noyis and schowte" are finally "so hiddowis" that the narrator awakens.

The other Damian poem, "Lucina schynnyng," emphasizes a similar use of the conventional, though here, instead of employing the allegorical, Dunbar emphasizes the prophetic. In a dream his narrator hears Fortune tell him that he will not have any profit until an abbot clothes himself in eagle's feathers and flies up in the air (23–24). Although the narrator had thought this a foolish dream, he is joyful at the end to hear that this improbable event is about to occur—" 'Adew,' quod I, 'My drery dayis ar done' " (47). In the prophecy Damian's flight is clothed in mythological and apocalyptic garb:

> He sall ascend as ane horrebble grephoun,
> Him meit sall in the air ane scho dragoun;
> Thir terrible monsteris sall togidder thrist,
> And in the cludis gett [beget] the Antechrist,
> Quhill all the air infeck of thair pusoun.

Under Saturnus fyrie regioun
Symone Magus sall meit him, and Mahoun,
And Merlyne at the mone sall him be bydand [awaiting]
And Jonet the weido on ane bussome [broom] rydand,
Off wichis with ane windir garesoun [wondrous company].
(26-35)[38]

Such references not only serve to evaluate Damian's activity, they give it a mock gravity that causes it to appear additionally ludicrous.

Damian's folly creates the tone of both of these poems as Dunbar treats him as a fool and as an obvious object of ridicule and contempt. Damian is essentially different from Donald Owre, however, who, in Dunbar's view, was evil, not ludicrous. While it is likely that Dunbar would have preferred James to get rid of Damian, any such hopes are subordinate to his poems; they are neither what the poems are about nor what they are aimed at. The *Epetaphe*, however, is aimed at effecting the death of Donald Owre.

Along with writing of court figures and of figures significant to the court, and along with celebrating the occasions pertinent to it, Dunbar frequently referred, sometimes in detail, to the ways of the court. His satire, "Thir ladyis fair, That makis repair" (no. 48) is as much a criticism of the court—king's court and law court both—as it is of the ladies who, frequenting the court, can do more to settle a dispute in three evenings than their husbands can do in ten days (3–5).[39] These "ladyis fair" (1), also called "ladyis wyis" [wise] (45), receive on a literal level only praise from the poet. Dunbar's scorn is directed more at the court that permits such goings on and at the lords who allow their wives to solicit on their behalf (21–24). Although the poet shows no overt anger, his bitter mockery is easy to see, intensified by the lightly tripping meter and the internal rhyme that makes the lines seem even shorter than they are. Everything seems light, gay, and sophisticated; and the result, a piece of criticism made with a pleasant smile, is no less effective than others made with a whip or bludgeon. Although for purposes of criticism Dunbar most commonly prefers wild comic invective, he shows here his ability to handle another method of satire.

The law court, specifically the Court of Session, where civil suits were heard, is the subject of another more detailed satire, "Ane murlandis man of uplandis mak" (no. 43).[40] Ostensibly a report of news from the Session, the poem is an overt indictment of the hypocrisy, dissimulation, and greed that mark this court and those who come to it. The corruption of secular and religious alike is apparent in this topsy-turvy place where no one acts as expected or with reason. Religious men, for instance, come to the court to see and woo fair faces, to engender and beget more friars, and are "unmyndfull of thair professioun" (43–47), that is, probably, forgetful of the vows they have taken. What is worse, the corruption is contagious: "The yungar at the eldar leiris" (48).

It would be difficult to consider either this poem or "Thir ladyis fair" as designed to amuse a court audience. Dunbar's satire is that of the moralist, not that of the entertainer. Any doubt that these poems reflect on the king's court will be removed by examining the so-called *Rewl of Anis Self* (no. 41, title from Hailes). Apparently addressing a would-be courtier, Dunbar presents in the opening lines a concise statement of his theme: "To dwell in court, my freind, gife that thow list [wish], / For gift of fortoun invy thow no degre" (1–2). That is, if one wishes to live in court, he must take care not to desire the gifts of fortune. As the refrain states this thought, "He rewlis weill, that weill him self can gyd" (8). The court would seem to be the great corrupter, leading one astray. Not only a microcosm of the world, it is more precisely a place of corruption and hypocrisy—the double, as it were, of the Session seen earlier. Although the advice here may seem "Polonius-like" and banal,[41] Dunbar's point is, first, that in court one cannot trust appearances—"trewth dwellis nocht ay for that trewth appeiris" (10); and, second, that in court, where many things are "variand," one must strive to hold firm to God: "Hald God thy freind, evir stabill be him stand, / He will the confort in all misaventeur" (43–44).[42]

If these moralizings about life at court are directed at a particular audience, it surely must be the king, who, though not directly responsible for the corruption around him, must most of all, if he is to rule well, hold fast to God and lead a good life. The king is actually mentioned in "Be divers wyis and operatiounes" (no. 29),[43] where, after presenting a list of the machinations of those seeking preferment at court, the poet refers to "the Kyngis grace" (24) and to his own trust in this. The "divers wyis and operatiounes" listed in this poem are hardly laudatory. Besides "service and diligence" (3)—suggesting that Dunbar's view of court was a balanced one—the methods of those seeking preferment range from singing, dancing, and storytelling (7) to feigning, flattering, and playing the fool (9–10); and these ploys are what the poem emphasizes. This uncom-

plimentary picture of court life culminates in a study of the covetousness of the soliciters:

> Sum beris [acts] as he wald ga wud [go mad]
> For hait desyr off warldis gud;
> Sum at the mes leves all devocion,
> And besy labouris for premocione.
>
> (15–18)

In contrast to such proceedings, the poet writes that he knows no
way of acting but to commend himself to the king's grace "with ane
humill cheir and face" (23). More than criticizing those who view
worldly gain as the whole of their life, Dunbar presents what has
been termed "a curious picture of the court of James the Fourth";[44]
and, indeed, the picture is close to that given by Chaucer in the
House of Fame, when he describes the seekers after fame. It would
seem that James is being called upon to show that he is above all this
greed and folly and that he can judge and act wisely.

Related to this poem is "Schir, ye have mony servitouris" (no.
17).[45] Also in octosyllabic couplets, this poem gives an even fuller
picture of the court, suggesting more strongly than the previous one
that it is a Vanity Fair to be shunned by all honest men. Beginning
with a long list of the "mony servitouris / And officiaris" (1–2) at
court—including "Musicianis, menstralis, and mirrie singaris"
(9)—the poet goes on to distinguish these "gudlie wichtis" (8) from
those hangers-on who are not deserving: "Fenyeouris, fleichouris,
and flatteraris; /Cryaris, craikaris, and clatteraris; /Soukaris, grou-
karis, gledaris, gunnaris (39–41).[46] And so it goes for many lines as
Dunbar lists the parasites, fools, and hypocrites who too frequently
are successful in receiving the king's favors. When the poet sees
these creatures being rewarded, he cannot contain himself—"Than
on this fals world I cry, Fy!" (68)—and his heart nearly breaks at
seeing "So grit abusioun . . . Daylie in court befoir myn E!" (71–72).
Whether or not Dunbar is wholly serious in his request for preferment—here where he threatens to "lat the vennim ische all out" (85)
unless there be some remedy, his attitude is unclear—he is certainly clear in his presentation of the corruption at court and in his
concern about it.[47] Although he elsewhere presents the court in a
humorous and joking manner, his view of it is ultimately serious and
critical.

This critical attitude may be the basis of Dunbar's humorous presentation of sexual encounters, as seen in "This hindir nycht in

Dumfermeling" (no. 27) and "In secreit place this hyndir nycht" (no. 28). Although it is not definite that either of these poems is a satire of court life, both were probably designed for the amusement of the court. Whereas the former poem is called in the Bannatyne manuscript *The Wowing of the King quhen he was in Dumfermling*, this authority cannot be trusted. There is nothing in this story of a fox trying to seduce a lamb that necessarily refers to the king. As Baxter writes, "This is not the only place where Bannatyne has implicated King James without the confirmation of internal evidence, and his titles are not always even probable."[48] At the same time, it may be argued, first, that the efficient cause of these poems, especially of "This hindir nycht in Dumfermeling," was most likely some event known to the court—an event like the attempted flight which provided an occasion for the Damian poems—and, second, that these two pieces were written for the amusement of a court audience. In any case, Dunbar's attitude here cannot be called one of approval. His humor may be compared to his praise of the lady solicitors (no. 48) or of the black lady (no. 37); his tone may be like that seen in a poem apparently addressed to the queen: "Madam, your men said thai wald ryd" (no. 31).[49]

The setting is "Fasterrennis evin," Shrove Tuesday, known best today as Mardi Gras, a traditional night of celebrating and feasting before the beginning of Lent. Although, says Dunbar, the men said they would ride, their wives bade them stay home and "lib tham of the pockis" (5), that is, apparently, cure themselves of venereal disease—the phrase, especially the term "pockis," providing a refrain for the seven stanzas of the poem. The joke would seem to be the idea that the cure of the "pox" lay in sexual intercourse—this is doubtless what Dunbar refers to at the end of the poem as "that perrellous play, / That men callis libbin of the pockis" (34–35). As in "This hindir nycht in Dumfermeling," Dunbar plays with animal imagery. The lusty men prove not to be "cockis" (8); they who had been "ryatous as rammis" are made tame "lyk ony lammis" (16–17); they settle down like sorry old ewes, "sarye crockis" (18); and, continuing this sheep imagery, their wives are described as coming forth "in flockis" (3).[50] Dunbar's criticism of wrong loving, though unstated, is obvious enough; and even though this poem might well function as court entertainment, its humor is only on the surface. Like so much humorous medieval verse—including perhaps Dunbar's other sexual poems—its essential point is a wholly serious one.

One final poem, "We that ar heir in hevins glory" (no. 30), may help us to understand even more clearly Dunbar's existence as court poet. Called *Dunbaris dirige to the King* in the Redpeith manuscript, *The Dregy of Dunbar maid to King James the fyift* [*sic*] in Bannatyne, and *Dunbarris Derige of Edinburgh and Striuiling* in the Asloane manuscript, the only point of agreement in all these versions is that the poem is a dirge, more accurately, a parody of parts of the Office of the Dead. Beyond this it is not clear to whom the poem is addressed. Baxter says that Bannatyne's James V must be rejected because this king-to-be would have been too young at any time the poem could have been written; and, even though there is no direct reference to the king here, the work is probably addressed to James IV, an identification apparently first made by Pinkerton in 1786—although Baxter worries that "to exalt the joys of Edinburgh in the King's absence may be considered lacking in tact."[51] The poem is now interpreted as Dunbar's attempt to lure the king from the seclusion of the Franciscan convent at Stirling— presented as a "panefull purgatory"—back to "the blis and glory / Off Edinburgh, the mirry toun: (19–21)—presented as "parradyis" (4). But whatever its particular occasion, its language would suggest that it is most likely addressed to several people, not to only one person. At the beginning, "we" folk in Edinburgh are contrasted with "yow" in Stirling (4–6); the poet also addresses "ye heremeitis and hankersaidilis [anchorites]" (9); and the Latin employs plural pronouns and nouns in reference to those in Stirling (107–10). In fact, the poem takes the form of a humorous comparison between the sinners and the saved; and any attempt to see it as a direct address to James is to make it be something it is not, and perhaps to alter its ultimate meaning.

Resembling "I, Maister Andro Kennedy" in its outrageous use of Latin religious phrases, it is also like this poem in being a conscious study in folly, and like several other poems of the late Middle Ages that parody the Mass—Skelton's *Philip Sparrow* is a notable contemporary example.[52] To think that Dunbar's poem—or the others in the tradition—is sacrilegious or blasphemous [53] is to misunderstand medieval parody. Such parody was possible because the truths being presented were beyond doubt and were certainly not to be endangered by being presented in terms of something unworthy or inappropriate. Indeed, the parody functions not to mock the Church or God, but to suggest the ideal behind the inadequate given. What is being laughed at is not the religious ideal but its unworthy worldly expression. Only from an inadequate understanding of reality could the court be described seriously as "hevins glory" (1) and "parradyis" (4). This obvious exaggeration suggests that the poem is well within the medieval tradition that saw humor in the praise of that which did not deserve praise. Ultimately such praise becomes a way of criticism, and so it is here.

Not only is the language exaggerated, the whole view of reality presented in this poem is a topsy-turvy one. As the speaker presents his argument, those who are being religious recluses, who have gone off from the world and given up its values, should cease their "pennance" and "abstinence" (88) and return to the paradise of pleasure represented by the court to "play, sing, and dance / Heir in to Edinburch" (68–69). They should leave behind spiritual sustenance and immerse themselves in the food of this world:

> Ye may in hevin heir with us dwell,
> To eit swan, cran, pertrik, and plever [plover],
> And every fische that swymis in rever;
> To drynk with us the new fresche wyne,
> That grew upoun the rever of Ryne,
> Fresche fragrant clairettis out of France,
> Of Angers and of Orliance,
> With mony ane cours of grit dyntie [dainty]:
> Say ye amen for cheritie.
>
> (50–58)

This presentation of heaven in terms of pleasures ordinarily associated with gluttony makes the irony obvious, as does the last line with its use in such a context of the significant religious terms "amen" and "cheritie." The passage may also be calling up Satan's temptation of Christ, who had been fasting in the wilderness, with the food of this world.[54]

As the narrator presents it, Stirling, with its religious retreat, is "every court manis fo" (34); and from the courtier's inadequate point of view the court at Edinburgh is paradise. When Dunbar stresses over and over that the penitents will find in Edinburgh "joy and blis," as well as "wirschep, welth, and weilfar," and "Pley, plesance, and eik honesty" (35–37), he is presenting a view diametrically opposed to the criticism he leveled against the city in his poem addressed to the merchants of Edinburgh (no. 44), as well as to the adverse judgment he voiced against the court in such poems as *Rewl of Anis Self* (no. 41) and *Tydingis fra the Sessioun* (no. 43).

The inverted picture here presents Stirling first as an unpleasant purgatory (19), then as a place of "distres" (43), of "panis fell [cruel]" (49) and "panis soir" (86), and finally as "hiddous hell" (94), that is, as something completely different from purgatory, for in hell no souls may be purged of their sins. The confusion here is in accord with the distorted view of the narrator that sees paradise on earth, especially in the court.

The emphasis on purgatory may be relevant to the time of year, called up later in the poem when Dunbar tells those in Stirling to "tak in patience / Your pennance and your abstinence, / And ye sall cum, or Yule begyn" into bliss (87–90), suggesting the forty days of fasting before Christmas, a period of time commonly referred to as Martinmas Lent. In terms of such a reference it is additionally ironic for the narrator to identify himself as "the angell Sanct Gabriell" (74). Not only a link between purgatory and paradise, Gabriel also functions in the Annunciation as the herald of man's salvation.[55]

The Office of the Dead parodied here, though designed to bring souls from purgatory to paradise, may function ultimately as a lament for the court, the place of real death. Dunbar the court poet may ultimately and essentially be Dunbar the court critic, who speaks out through both humor and invective against its inadequacies and excesses. The differences between Dunbar the court entertainer and Dunbar the moralist would seem finally to be more superficial than real.

CHAPTER 4

The Christian Moralist

I *Mutability and Death*

WHAT has been suggested several times in the course of this analysis of Dunbar is that at the heart of his poems—no matter whether they are in the form of humorous banterings, grotesqueries, celebrations, or allegories—lies a moral sense that ultimately views everything human in terms of eternal values and ultimate truths. Although literature today may easily be separated into the religious and the secular, in the Middle Ages, including early sixteenth-century Scotland, such a dichotomy was neither apparent nor real. That is, the distinction would not have been a meaningful one to Dunbar or to his audience. In like manner, though we might prefer literature which is humorous to that which is didactic, in Dunbar's time the humor would most properly be found on the surface of the poem and exist as a way of arriving at doctrinal truth. The bare truth, without its clothing of fiction and poetic language, may be fine for those able to appreciate it, and the fit province of homiletic literature; but for many people the surface, with all its various attractions, is necessary if they are to arrive at this truth.

Along with writing subtle fictions, Dunbar also presented truth in overtly didactic homilies. Some of these—like the three "discretioun" pieces and like those poems emphasizing the need for man to be content with what he has[1]—have already been touched on. But many other overt moralizings state his main themes of the instability and transitoriness of human life and the world, the inadequacy of conventional institutions, and the perverseness of man who, though able to change his sinful way of living, will not do so. None of these themes is original with Dunbar; they are the truths of his religion, and in stating them the poet provides man with guideposts on his journey through life. At the same time, in some of the poems treating these themes, the poet makes a particularly effective, even a memorable, statement.

"I that in heill wes and gladnes" (no. 7), for instance, is a deceptively simple piece. Its four-line stanza—rhyming in couplets, each line having four stresses, with the last line forming the refrain—is one of Dunbar's favorite stanzas, being used by him in ten other poems; but it is also, as Scott points out, "a very powerful little stanza, heroic in its stark elemental force, elegaic [*sic*] in its simplicity of statement, its solemnity."[2] Because each stanza is end-stopped, the thought is necessarily self-contained; and because one-quarter of each stanza is taken up by the refrain, only three lines may be used to state and develop this thought. Of necessity, the point of each stanza, and of the entire poem, is more simple than complex and is presented in a way that is more direct than indirect. The main method of development is incremental repetition—a favorite device of such popular verse forms as ballads—where one stanza may, in effect, restate the thought of the previous stanza while varying or adding to it. The repetition—seen most immediately in the refrain—allows the point to be driven home; the variations and additions permit the widest application of the point.

In "I that in heill wes and gladnes," the first twelve stanzas discuss mutability in general. Stanzas 1–4 state with several variations that transitoriness is the way of the world. Stanza 5, saying that "to the ded gois all Estatis, / Princis, Prelotis, and Potestatis, / Baith riche and pur of al degre" (17–19), provides a transition from the general to the more particular. Stanzas 6–11 list mainly by occupation—knights, clerks, physicians, etc.—those who might have been able to, but in actuality cannot, defeat or outwit death. With stanza 12 a transition is made as Dunbar focuses on the English and Scottish poets who have died; and stanzas 13–23 list these men, from "noble Chaucer, of makaris flour" (50) to Kennedy on his deathbed, and finally to Dunbar himself, who realizes that he is next in line as death's prey (95). The final stanza states the conclusion that must necessarily be drawn from this incremental repetition:

> Sen for the deid remeid is none,
> Best is that we for dede dispone [dispose],
> Eftir our deid that lif may we;
>   *Timor mortis conturbat me.*

                                                                    (97–100)

This is the moral of the entire poem, that which builds on the point, presented over and over in explicit statement and exemplum, that "This fals warld is bot transitory" (6).

Rather than try to conceal the repetition, Dunbar if anything goes out of his way to emphasize it. The syntax is by and large paratactic, employing coordinate rather than subordinate constructions. Sentences are paralleled: "Our plesance heir is all vane glory, / This fals warld is bot transitory, / The flesche is brukle, the Fend is sle" (5–7). Words within sentences are likewise paralleled: "The state of man dois change and vary, / Now sound, now seik, now blith, now sary, / Now dansand mery, now like to dee" (9–11). While the contrast between good and bad is here emphasized, parallelism is stressed by the anaphoric repetition of "now." Not only are verbs and adjectives paralleled, so are nouns: death "takis the campion in the stour [fight], / The capitane closit in the tour, / The lady in bour full of bewte" (29–31). Brought about by this parallelism is the impression of both incremental repetition and cataloging; and, indeed, in its listing of dead poets the poem becomes in effect a catalog.

In the last two stanzas, however, both beginning with "Sen", the overall structure of the poem is revealed as hypotactic. That is, as Dunbar writes, "since" death is the way of the world, I see I cannot escape it (93–96); and "since" this is the case, everyone should prepare for death, prepare, in effect, by living properly, so that he may live afterward (97–100). But even with this final sense that the overall movement is one of cause and effect, the parataxis, mainly the listing, is what is dominant. Because we know in essence what each stanza is saying and will say, we are aware mostly of the accumulation, the accretion, that is the proving of the poet's point.

Notwithstanding the personal application of the first and the penultimate stanzas, the dominant impression here is that Dunbar is fully in control of his material, working artfully to give the impression of artlessness and simplicity. It may have been his intention to have the twenty-five stanzas comprising the poem speak of twenty-five poets, including himself, and to arrive purposefully at a total of one hundred lines, suggesting perhaps, like the hundred cantos of Dante's *Divine Comedy*, totality and perfection.

The cataloging and development by repetition found here are Dunbar's main methods in those poems of his that are generally classified as moralizings.[3] The term is an unfortunate one, first, because today at least it has undesirable connotations, and, second,

because it may imply that his moral concern is to be found only in
these poems. In general these poems are straightforward statements
of moral truth, though they range in form from musings about
mutability and sin to exhortations and advice about living well.
Overtly didactic, they state their point directly and there is no
misunderstanding it. "I that in heill wes and gladnes" is like them in
some of its passages, especially in its last stanza; but in its personal
application and in its listing of the dead poets it becomes more
oblique than direct.

A good example of Dunbar's moralizings is provided by the piece
commonly called *Of the Warldis Instabilitie* (no. 13), the first stanza
of which reveals its substance and method:

> This waverand warldis wretchidnes,
> The failyeand and frutless bissines,
> The mispent tyme, the service vane,
> For to considder is ane pane.

(1–4)

Not only does the poem present the same theme as "I that in heill
wes and gladnes," it employs the same paralleling and cataloging,
the same stanzaic form, and the same number of stanzas and lines. It
too makes a personal application of the uncertainty it states and
restates, though its apparent appeal to the king, may be, as has been
seen, more a literary device than an efficient cause.

Another poem known as *Of Lyfe* (no. 76) indicates further the
nature of Dunbar's moralizings. In the form of a single Chaucerian
stanza, it may be quoted in its entirety:

> Quhat is this lyfe bot ane straucht way to deid,
>   Quhilk hes a tyme to pas, and nane to duell;
> A slyding quheill us lent to seik remeid;
>   A fre chois gevin to Paradice or Hell;
> 5 A pray to deid, quhome vane is to repell;
>   A schoirt torment for infineit glaidnes,
>   Als schort ane joy for lestand hevynes.

Essentially a definition, the poem first gives the impression of being
in the form of a question, then of a question and answer; but its
answers, understandable though they may be, also create a sense of
ambiguity. Seeing life as but a means to an end, not as an end in

itself, man may reach that which is beyond life; for man to view life as an end, that is, for him to look for joy here in this world, is for him to find "lestand hevynes." Man should regard life, first, as a place of sorrow, a "schoirt torment" that can bring "infineit glaidnes," and, second, as a pathway to something else that is permanent and good.

The medieval view of life as a state of pilgrimage is brought out most clearly by Dunbar in "O wreche, be war! this warld will wend the fro" (no. 75)[4] where the point is made, with intentional ambiguity, that if man does not leave the world, it will leave him: "Walk furth, pilgrame, quhill thow hes dayis lycht, / Dres fra desert, draw to thy duelling place; / Speid home, for quhy [because] anone cummis the nicht." (9–11). The transitory world is a "desert," a place where nothing is "stabill" or firm (17); it is man's "cruell fo" (20), even "the deith" (14) for those who abide in it. The refrain from Ecclesiastes—"Vanitas Vanitatum, et omnia Vanitas"—not only punctuates the point made in each of the poem's three stanzas, it also acts as a final definition of the world and provides a basis for the sense of urgency created by the imperative mood of the poem. From the opening "O wreche, be war!" each of the sentences is in the form of a command; and the dominant word of the last stanza is "now," again emphasizing the sense of immediacy.

The play of Latin against English suggested here is even more significant in "Memento, homo, quod cinis es!" (no. 74),[5] where the opening line, as well as the refrain, "Quod tu in cinerem reverteris," is based on the Ash Wednesday service as found in the Sarum Missal; and again the Latin provides a final definitive word and allows another form of repetition. The first line is translated and echoed in the English that follows—"Think, man, thow art bot erd and as!" (2)—and the refrain that man will become dust again, most often preceded by the repeated command for man to "think," is anticipated and prepared for both by particular lines in the stanza—"For as thow come sa sall thow pas" (4)—and by the thought developed in each stanza.

After the first stanza the idea of mutability is reaffirmed by means of the medieval *Ubi sunt?* convention. All the worthy, strong, noble, humble, and fair heroes of the past have "playit thair pairtis, and all are gone" (13). The poet insists, "Think, man, exceptioun thair is none" (15). In stanza 3, this changes to an *Ubi erunt?* theme. Man is asked to realize that he may be "within ane yeir, / Ane ugsum, uglye tramort" (19–20), that is, a repulsive, ugly corpse. The insistence on this necessary fate continues through the remainder of the poem as man is assured that "The dragone Death that all devouris" (28) will swallow him, and the poem ends with the hope that even though the body will be lost, the soul may ultimately be kept alive with Christ (45–47). In its application of the traditional *memento mori* motif, in which man is reminded that life must be seen in the context of death, along with the *Ubi sunt?* and *Ubi erunt?* themes, the poem may seem to be a hodgepodge of conventions and commonplaces. Still, through its vivid images, incremental repetition, and sense of immediacy—the result largely of the direct address—the poem is more than a piece of traditional advice. Although the moralizing is overt, and although the poet speaks by and large with the voice of the preacher, the progress of the poetic line is compelling.

Dunbar's success here is due not only to his command of imagery, meter, and sound patterns, and not only to his skill with rhetoric and various devices of cataloging, but more particularly to his blending end-stopped lines with intricately developed stanzas. Begun with or containing subordinating conjunctions—most notably "thocht" (17, 33, 42), meaning "though," chosen perhaps because of its sound relationship to "think"—each stanza contains in effect a single thought that leads to the conclusion of the refrain, "tu in cinerem reverteris." The fact that the preceding conjunction in this refrain varies—*Quod* (8, 24, 32, 40) *Sed* (16), *Cum* (48)—shows that the end-stopped lines with their built-in effect of parataxis are ultimately part of a hypotactic construction culminating in the reason found in the Latin: "you will return to dust." Moreover, in spite of the apparent directness of the lines, the poem is full of the indirectness provided necessarily by similies (5, 26), hypothetical situations (7), exempla (9), metonymy (25), and allegorical personifications (28). Even Christ at the end is presented obliquely as "Thy Ransonner with woundis fyve" (45); man should make him his "plycht anker" and his "steiris" (46), his principal anchor and helmsman, so as to avoid arriving in "deathis port" (42). This collection of mixed metaphors and methods—entirely justifiable in a poetry that views all surface detail as properly subordinated to theme—functions finally to provide a statement that goes beyond the trite and the commonplace.

While celebrating the truths and ideals of Christianity and providing men with assistance on their journey to salvation, Dunbar was also being a poetic artist; and, as with all medieval poets, no real distinction can be made between the role of the artist and that of the moralizer. Sometimes Dunbar the moralizer uses rather incongruously but intentionally the conventions of the court poet, as in *All Erdly Joy Returnis in Pane* (no. 71), when he employs a bird as his spokesman. Far from being an ordinary courtly dream vision, praise of spring, or fable, this poem cites the facts of mutability. Their being uttered by a bird, far from lessening their validity, casts doubt on the typical employment of birds in poetry. Words like "Deth followis lyfe with gaipand mowth, / Devoring fruct and flowring grane" (10–11) do not commonly come from the beaks of birds in medieval courtly literature. Although the references to fruit and grain might seem appropriate, the moral sentiment itself would never have been uttered by the birds of Chaucer's *Parliament of Fowls* or *Squire's Tale,* or, for that matter, of Dunbar's *Thrissil and the Rois,* that are traditionally associated with spring, joy, and earthly love.

As the first lines of the poem make clear, the time is Lent, and the subject is man's salvation:

> Off Lentren in the first mornyng,
> Airly as did the day up spring,
> Thus sang ane bird with voce upplane [rustic],
> "All erdly joy returnis in pane."
>
> (1–4)

Although Lent is used elsewhere in Middle English poetry as a synonym for spring, as in the lyrics beginning "Lenten ys come with loue to toune, / With blosmen and with briddes roune, / That al this blisse bryngeth";[6] and although the bird's song here would seem to make such an identification possible, Dunbar obviously has in mind the Christian sense of Lent, the period of penance and abstinence before Easter. Throughout the poem, through the emphasis on mutability, courtly and allegorical conventions are put in a proper context—"Come nevir yit May so fresche and grene, / Bot Januar come als wod and kene" (17–18). The joys and beauties of spring are seen in the context of winter, which is more accurately the condition of this life. So it is with every apparent worldly good and pleasure; not only do they not last, they act to bring about their opposites (25–28). If Dunbar was at all aware of numerological significance, he might consciously have written this poem and others like it in four-line stanzas, with four stresses per line, since four was the tradi-tional number of this world and things associated with it. Moreover, that there are ten such stanzas here may likewise be purposeful, since ten was the most frequent number of perfection or fulfillment; and the total number of lines, forty, may be significant as repre-senting both the number of days in Lent and a symbolic period of testing.[7]

Another poem employing the same stanzaic and metrical form is "Man, sen thy lyfe is ay in weir" (no. 72),[8] where the premise is that the goods of this world are insidious for, in creating desire in man, they cause him to be in a state of sin. Although this poem may seem to differ in approach from the other moralizings, Dunbar is serious in emphasizing man's responsibility for seeing that his goods do not corrupt others. Whereas both spendthrifts and hoarders were tradi-tionally viewed as wrongly using the goods of this world—as may be seen strikingly in the late Middle English *Winner and Waster*, as well as in canto 7 of Dante's *Inferno*—Dunbar's view would seem to be that he who is concerned with gain is ultimately more dangerous than he who uses up earthly goods. Instead of preserving these goods, man should use them up so that when he is dead, no one may "ane uder slay nor chace" in order to gain them (13–16). The refrain, "Thyne awin gud spend quhill thow hes spais," reaffirms the point but also in its last four words emphasizes the transitoriness of life.

The theme of this poem is found in another form in the first stanza of "He that hes gold and grit riches" (no. 2),[9] where the person who has at his command earthly wealth but chooses to live in "wrechitnes" is regarded as perverse and as one who "wirkis sorrow to him sell" (1–5), this last phrase being the refrain of the piece. The theme is also seen in those moralizings of Dunbar that are specifically concerned with the necessity of man's being oblivious to the gifts of fortune, of his being "blyth" and "content" with what he has. The ideal would seem to be contained in the couplet, "Now all this tyme lat us be mirry, / And sett nocht by this warld a chirry."[10] It is not that one should strive for earthly goods but that one should use them well. As Dunbar notes elsewhere (no. 67), in much the same words, "Man, pleis thy makar and be mirry, / And sett not by this warld a chirry"; but he then goes on to state his real point: Man should not seek earthly goods, but should "Wirk for the place of paradyce."[11]

II *Sin and the Human Situation*

Closely related to these relatively straightforward moralizings are those poems reflecting the very human concern with one's reputation and the impossibility of acting in such a way as to please all men. In "Musing allone this hinder nicht" (no. 8),[12] the point is that even though everyone will be judged (5), it is not man who is the proper or trustworthy judge. The narrator trusts that "with Goddis grace," he will have a place in heaven, "For thair sall no man demit be" (51–55). The irony lies in the intermingling of the judgments of man and of God and the play on "deming" in the sense of judgment and censure. Man's "demings" are everywhere but mean nothing; God's "deming," at the end of life and world—at Doomsday—is the only one to count, and it is only through this one that man can finally get beyond judgment.

The poem is unusual in the situation it projects. In the first stanza the narrator appears at night, "quhen gone was licht," within a garden under a tree musing alone about "mirry day." He then hears "ane voce" say "May na man now undemit be," as well as the substance of the next ten stanzas that comprise the poem. The voice, like that of the bird in "Off Lentren in the first mornyng" (no. 71), is out of place in this garden setting; but the musing has led to the audial equivalent of a vision, which in effect contradicts and shows the error of man's concern with "mirry day." His proper concern should be not earthly joy or sorrow but the "deming" that all men will of necessity receive. And while the poem may include contemporary particulars—life at court (21), the view of James IV (46)—these are subordinate to the ultimate truth it brings out.

The idea of the poem, found also in the late Middle Ages in Chaucer's ballade *Truth* and in Lydgate's *A Wicked Tongue Will Say Amiss*, is traditional, although the treatment here is unusual. A more standard and more immediately comprehensible treatment of the theme appears in Dunbar's "How sould I rewill me or in quhat wys" (no. 9),[13] whose conclusion is that since he cannot hope that his actions will satisfy other men, the poet will ignore "mannis toung" and "do the best" he can (47–48), trusting finally that "The gratious God mot governe me" (50).

Implicit in both of these poems is criticism of the particular judgments of the world and, moreover, of the ability of man to judge in any responsible way. In line with what Chaucer had depicted in the

House of Fame the poet prefers to know himself what his worth is. In his view the voice of the world cannot be trusted and should not be valued. Its pronouncements are too frequently based on jealousy, envy, and hypocrisy, and too often changeable. The world is more properly criticized than consulted or valued; and several of Dunbar's moralizings function actually as satires of the world and of those who embrace it.

While it may be true that Dunbar was "not primarily a satirist,"[14] he still wrote many satires. Sometimes these focus on particular institutions, such as the law courts in *Tydingis fra the Sessioun* (no. 43). At other times they show the inadequacy of religious institutions, as in "This nycht, befoir the dawing cleir" (no. 4) with its criticism of friars. The "mony wrink and wyle," trick and guile (42), associated with friars are hardly preferable to the corruption of secular institutions; and when the narrator will not accept his visitant's command to "Reffus the warld, for thow mon be a frier" (5), the point seems to be that denying the world is not in itself a solution. What one replaces the world with must be taken into account.

Dunbar lashes out at corruption in general in "Doverrit with dreme, devysing in my slummer" (no. 77),[15] and again his main method is cataloging. After the first stanza, which sets the criticism in a dream, the poet notes how the realm has changed from prosperity to adversity. And the next fifteen stanzas, through the repetition of "sic" (such) and "so many," list the various corruptions to be found. The stanzas commonly pile up a series of noun phrases that act as subject of the sentence, which is then finished in the refrain, "Within this land was nevir hard nor sene"—that is, the corruptions were never seen before now. The method and phrasing are strikingly like those of a poem, *The Manner of the World Nowadays,* formerly attributed to Dunbar's English contemporary John Skelton. This poem also begins its sentences with the "So many" construction and has as refrain the phrase "Saw I never."[16] Rather than there being any direct relationship between these two works, however, it is more likely that both are part of a late medieval satiric genre that viewed contemporary vice and corruption in the light of a perfect society.

The only sense of development in the cataloging of corruption in "Doverrit with dreme" occurs at the end where the sinners described are pejoratively referred to as being "Off Sathanis senyie," Satan's court (79). But the freedom provided by the apparently random selection of detail may allow for the prosodic intricacy here, one that is unusual even for Dunbar. One stanza will serve to illustrate this complexity:

> Sa mony lordis, so mony naturall fulis,
> That better accordis to play thame at the trulis [bowls(?)],
> Nor seis the dulis [trouble] that commonis dois sustene;
> New tane fra sculis sa mony anis [asses] and mulis
> Within this land was nevir hard nor sene.
>
> (21–25)

Rhyme is employed not only at the end of lines but at the end of half lines—"lordis" and "accordis," "dulis" and "sculis,"—and these latter terms rhyme also with the end words "fulis," "trulis," and "mulis." The sets of rhymes continue with "sustene" and "sene." Sixteen such stanzas make the piece a *tour de force* of rhyme and may well make us wonder which was more important to Dunbar, content or form. It is as though the subject of the world's corruption provided a sufficiently large stage for his craft to express itself in full.[17]

The vices of the world are detailed more specifically in "This nycht in my sleip I wes agast" (no. 42),[18] another dream vision in which the poet is, as it were, given insight into the nature of sin, in particular sin that has profanity as its basis. The setting is the marketplace of this world through which the devil passes recruiting sinners, saying to them as he hears their curses, "Renunce thy God and cum to me." Again Dunbar's method is essentially one of cataloging, but here may be a real progression of detail in that the social classes are cited in descending order of respectability. The textual problems of the poem do not interfere with our understanding either its general point or its overall structure.[19] Beginning with priest and courtier who blaspheme God with "aithis of crewaltie" (3), the poem proceeds through the middle-class craftsmen, those who lie about the merit of their products, to dicer and thief, those, that is, who are wastrels and predators, showing each in turn damning himself with his oaths. The device Dunbar uses is such that the action proceeds as in a pageant, and there is no need for authorial comment or explicit criticism of the sinners.

Similar to this work is "Off Februar the fyiftene nycht" (no. 57—called by Samuel Marion Tucker "perhaps Dunbar's most remarkable poem"[20]—where again the narrator is seen having a dream, though in this case he lies specifically in a "trance" (3), a state, it would seem, between life and death. But instead of hearing the voices of sinners, in this poem the narrator sees the sinners performing a dance. Or, rather, the various particular sinners are here subsumed under the figures of the Deadly Sins. Since each sin has its adherents dancing with it, the stage is even more crowded than the marketplace was in the previously discussed poem. Fastern's Eve again provides the time of the dream, and the dance, called in hell by Mahoun (7), is in some respects the equivalent of the sexual encounters on Fastern's Eve detailed in "Madam, your men said thai wald ryd" (no. 31) and perhaps provides a basis for understanding the irony of that work. Here the dance that Mahoun commands the gallants to begin is to be in the latest French fashion (12)—a touch that may recall the *Dance in the Quenis Chalmer* and suggest additional irony there.

The Deadly Sins appear individually, each contained in a single twelve-line stanza which not only describes the sin, but presents it further in terms of its human manifestations and its consequences. Pride, for instance, wearing ceremonial dress, has in his train "mony prowd trumpour," many a proud imposter, who dance through "skaldand fyre" grimacing with hideous groans (22–24). The dance here is a *danse macabre*, a study in both humor and horror, a dance that is essentially painful not pleasurable. Again, although basically in the form of a listing of sins, the poem is marked by vivid imagery and language. The picture of Covetousness, who enters after Envy, is typical of Dunbar's accomplishment here:

> Nixt him in dans come Cuvatyce,
> Rute of all evill and grund of vyce,
> That nevir cowd be content;
> Catyvis, wrechis, and ockeraris [usurers]
> Hud-pykis [misers], hurdaris [hoarders], and gadderaris
> All with that warlo [warlock] went:
> Out of thair throttis thay schot on udder
> Hett moltin gold, me thocht a fudder [great amount],
> As fyreflawcht [lightning] maist fervent;
> Ay as thay tomit [emptied] thame of schot,
> Feyndis fild thame new up to the thrott
> With gold of allkin prent.
>
> (55–66)

Covetousness is defined, then illustrated, then punished—or, more
precisely, taken to a point where it is seen being its own punishment.

The sinners accompanying the Sins are particularized only when
at the end Mahoun calls for a "Heleand padyane," a highland
pageant or perhaps a highland fling (109). Then the highlanders led
by Macfadden, a name probably chosen for its typicality,[21] begin to
chatter and croak so much in Gaelic that the devil, deafened by their
noise, smothers them with smoke in the deepest pit of hell (115–20).
Although Scott feels that this last stanza has "no obvious connexion
with the Deidly Synnis as such" and is "really a second poem in its
own right, in a sense" [*sic*],[22] it functions as the finale of the dance,
as that which presents in a single tangible and recognizable shape all
the sins hitherto seen separately and abstractly.

Two shorter six-line stanzas, which do not fit with the other nine
twelve-line stanzas in the poem, need comment.[23] The first of these
occurs after the second stanza, which describes the dance of Pride:

> Heilie [disdainful] harlottis on hawtane [haughty] wyis
> Come in with mony sindrie gyis [manner],
> Bot yit luche [laughed] nevir Mahoun,
> Quhill preistis come in with bair schevin nekkis,
> Than all the feyndis lewche and maid gekkis [mocking gestures],
> Blak Belly and Bawsy Brown.
>
> (25–30)

The second, found immediately before the final stanza, explains that
ordinarily no minstrels are to be found in hell:

> Na menstrallis playit to thame but dowt [without doubt],
> For glemen thair wer haldin owt,
> Be day and eik by nycht;
> Except a menstrall that slew a man,
> Swa till his heretage he wan,
> And entirt by breif [letter] of richt.
>
> (103–8)

Breaking up the action of the dance, these two stanzas in different
stanzaic form may very well be interpolations;[24] but, on the other
hand, they are clearly in the style of the other stanzas and reinforce
the particularizing given in the references to highlanders in the last

stanza. Moreover, the second of these, commenting on the lack of minstrels in hell, provides a reason for Mahoun to call for the highland pageant, here apparently to be regarded as the hellish equivalent of music.

If these stanzas are to be regarded as integral parts of the poem, it might be best to reconsider an emendation made by Laing and place the first six-line passage after the first stanza in which Mahoun commands the "gallandis" to begin the festivities. In spite of the likely connection of the "heilie harlottis" with Pride, this group differs from the others in that they are laughed at, not punished. The group contained in this six-line passage may more appropriately be seen entering before the dance-punishment begins, functioning, in effect, as a procession and leading to the first dancer, Pride. After this company has arrived, Mahoun can properly call for the dance: " 'Lat se,' quod he, 'Now quha begynnis' " (13). This six-line stanza, then, along with the first full twelve-line stanza, would function as the introduction to the dance and would parallel in structure the second six-line passage about minstrels in its relation to the last full stanza of the poem about the highlanders, and give a balanced frame to the dance.

Apparently related to the *Dance of the Sevin Deidly Synnis* is "Nixt that a turnament wes tryid" (no. 58).[25] In the Bannatyne manuscript the two poems are printed together without a break, and in the Maitland manuscript, though not contiguous with the *Dance*, the *Tournament* begins with its first and last stanzas. The two poems, moreover, reveal the same twelve-line stanziac form— though the meter is different—and, omitting the two short stanzas of the *Dance*, contain the same number of lines. Even though there is little doubt that the *Dance* and the *Tournament* represent two poems—besides being separated in Maitland, they are further distinguished by the existence of a sequel to the *Tournament*—still, the poems may most profitably be viewed as two expressions of the same overall conception and theme, with the narrator falling into a trance at the beginning of the *Dance* and not awakening until the end of the *Tournament*. Together the two poems may be seen as burlesques of the Shrove Tuesday merriment,[26] even perhaps suggesting what man's pre-Lent immersion in sin has as its anagogical correlative.

The poet's particular point in the two works is rather different. The *Dance*, with its real punishment of sin, gives way to the study in scatology found in the *Tournament*. The combat between tailor and cobbler ("sowtar") is not only a perversion of the knightly joust, it is also, with its anal imagery, a denigration of everything ostensibly noble and grave. The champions are hardly gentlemen; knighted by Mahoun, they function as a perversion of the concept of knight as soldier of Christ, *miles Christi*. These knights are afraid of each other, and they fight more with vomit, flatulence, and excrement than with knightly weapons, though their physical excesses are ironically described in courtly terms. When made a knight, the cobbler spews a quart of leather blacking over the devil's neck, repaying him, says Dunbar, in knightly fashion—"Thus knychtly he him quitt" (60). When the frightened jousters finally run together, the tailor, who befouls his saddle, is unseated. The cobbler's horse, frightened, runs to the Devil who turns his buttocks and rewards the cobbler well (78). The "new maid knychtis," lying "in swoun" and forswearing all arms, are finally cast into a dungeon by the Devil, deprived of knighthood, and made churls, a state, says the poet, they prefer (89–96). The poem ends with the narrator's laughing so hard at this good joke that he nearly bursts, and awakens from his "trance" (103).

The poem, like the Sir Thomas Norny piece with whose stanzaic form it has much in common, is clearly a satire against chivalry. It is just as clearly directed against the false imitators of chivalry, the would-be courtiers, also laughed at in the Middle English *Tournament of Tottenham* and the later Scots poem by Lindsay, *The Jousting between James Watson and John Barbour*.[27] But, most specifically, Dunbar seems to have chosen his adversaries, tailor and cobbler, because of what they represented for him and his audience. The reason for this choice is apparent when we look at the sequel to the *Tournament*, "Betuix twell houris and ellevin" (no. 59), known as the *Amends*.

In this work the poet dreams that "ane angell came fra Hevin" (2) to bless the tailors and cobblers and place them above all the saints "Nixt God grittest in dignitie" (7) because they "amend, / Be craft and grit agilitie" that which God "mismakkis" (10–11). They can so improve God's "misfassonit man" (25) that their product is better by three times than the original one (27). Because they perform such "mirakillis" on earth, they will be saints in heaven—though here they are considered knaves (37–39). The irony is obvious, but it is not that Dunbar harbored a personal grudge against these craftsmen or that his satire reflects the scorn of the courtiers directed at "the undistinguished crowd of humble artisans"[28] or that he wished "to ridicule trades whose tricks were disliked by the poet."[29] Rather, as clothes were seen to reflect, or conceal, man's real self, so their makers were viewed as imitating, or perverting, the Creator.[30] The tailored person in this sense is symbolic of the dissembler, and the tailors and cobblers, here praised for hiding human flaws, stand for those who provide the means of dissembling.

It is such a symbolic role that the tailor and "sowtar" play in Dunbar's complaint to the merchants of Edinburgh (no. 44), when he speaks of "Tailyouris, soutteris, and craftis vyll, / The fairest of your streitis dois fyll" (36–37). Also in "This nycht in my sleip I wes agast" (no. 42), tailor and cobbler appear at the beginning of the description of the middle-class craftsmen cursing in the mar-ketplace—and in all manuscripts of the poem the two stanzas de-scribing them are contiguous—thus setting the tone for what fol-lows. The tailor says that if there is a better-shaped gown in all the town, he will give himself to the Devil; and the cobbler says that the Devil may have him by the neck if better boots of leather are found to exist. In each case the words are obvious lies and the Devil gladly accepts their souls (31–40).

In the *Tournament* the tailor and cobbler—called contemptuously "A prick lous and ane hobbell clowttar" (5)—are to be seen as de-ceivers *par excellence* and clearly related to the Deadly Sins. In their tournament the deception they stand for is made manifest as they reveal their true natures. Although appearing to be knights, they are cowards. Whereas the point of the combat is never stated, the implication is that the winner will be he who is best able to deceive. When in the *Amends* Dunbar presents an angel blessing these figures, the irony implicit all along is made explicit. Moreover, the time of the dream, occurring as the first line says between twelve and eleven o'clock, may, in its suggestion of time's going backward, be a further indication of the *impossibilia* being presented here. Although the colophon in the Maitland manuscript suggests that the *Amends* may have been composed as an apology to the trade guilds—"Quod Dunbar quhone he drank to the dekynnis ffor amendis to the bodeis of thair craftis"[31]—it offers, with its obvi-ous humor, a strange kind of palinode. In fact, it is possible that the *Amends* was designed from the beginning to follow the *Tournament*. The two poems together may function as do the two pieces on James

Dog (nos. 33–34), although there the two are actually companion pieces whereas here the *Amends* most properly functions as an epilogue to the *Tournament* in the same way that the "*Respontio Regis*" provides an epilogue to "Now lufferis cummis" (no. 22).

III *Lent and Repentence*

Along with references to visions occurring on "this nycht"(nos. 4, 42) and "this hindir nycht" (nos. 8, 27, 28, 60), several of Dunbar's satires are associated with significant days in the Church calendar. Besides the poems clearly associated with Fastern's Eve (nos. 31, 57), others are related to Christmas (nos. 22, 23, 30) and to New Year's Day (nos. 26, 60). Another favorite day for Dunbar is Ash Wednesday, the day after Fastern's Eve and the first day of Lent. One poem calling up this date, "Off Lentren in the first mornyng" (no. 71), already discussed in terms of its employing a bird to instruct man about the transitoriness of earthly pleasure, uses the Lenten setting to make its instruction especially relevant. The first morning of Lent also provides the setting for a quite different kind of poem, known as the *Twa Cummeris* (no. 46).[32] Although the poem exists in various forms in four manuscripts, it may still be profitably examined in terms of its overall satire.[33] Representing far more than the "eternal ironic vision of the peasantry," or "an irreverent joke about Lent,"[34] or a satire against women,[35] especially against "the female sex of the lower classes, chiefly for their intemperance,"[36] or an example of "irresponsible irreverence with no moral undertone,"[37] the poem is an ironic statement of the misuse of this time of penance.

The first stanza—following the reading in the Bannatyne manuscript—sets the tone and method for the rest of the poem:

> Rycht airlie on Ask Weddinsday,
> Drynkand the wyne satt cumeris [gossips] tway;
> The tane [one] cowth to the tother complene,
> Graneand [groaning] and suppand [sipping] cowd scho say,
> "This lang Lentern makis me lene."
>
> (1–5)

The irony is obvious. The gossips are drinking wine on the first day of fasting; moreover, they are complaining on this first day about how long they have fasted, and, as is made clear, the speaker who so

complains is actually fat—"God wait [knows] gif scho wes grit and
fatt, / Yit to be feble scho did hir fene [feign]" (7–8). The subjects of
their discourse are drinking and sex. Wine, here functioning as food
of this world and the stuff of gluttony, may exist as a parody of wine
symbolizing in the Mass the spiritual food provided by Christ. Sex is
seen in the lust of one speaker, who voices her dissatisfaction with
her husband. And the poem is probably best read as a series of
alternating speeches between the representative of wine, or Gluttony, and that of sex, or Lechery. In this sense it would seem that
the personifications of these sins—seen allegorically in the *Dance of
the Sevin Deidly Sinnis*—are presenting their essential natures in
further detail.[38]

For all its apparent popularity and conscious structuring, the
poem seems in a sense incomplete. That is, the material is worth
more than the thirty lines Dunbar gives it; and, indeed, it may be
regarded as something of a first draft of the work known as the *Tretis
of the Tua Mariit Wemen and the Wedo* (no. 47).[39] But this longer
poem, perhaps Dunbar's finest effort, is only in part a satire against
overindulgence in the pleasures of this world; and it might just as
well be argued that the *Twa Cummeris* represents an isolated treatment of one aspect of the longer *Tretis*.

The ideal of Lent, so perverted in the *Twa Cummeris*, is the
explicit subject of the so-called *Maner of Passing to Confessioun* (no.
84). Beginning "O synfull man, thir ar the fourty dayis / That every
man sulde wilfull pennence dre" (1–2), it emphasizes the necessity
of penance. In the form of a sermon it offers advice about the need
for man to consider his sins carefully and acknowledge them with
proper humility and contrition. The work is a calm, rational statement without the passion or urgency found elsewhere in Dunbar's
moralizings,[40] and its sobriety contrasts with the frivolity seen as the
two "cummeris" continue their feasting even into Lent.

It is in the light of these satires that one of Dunbar's most interesting poems, commonly called the *Dream* (no. 60), should be
seen. Again in the form of a dream, more accurately, a state between sleep and waking—as the first line describes it, "This hinder
nycht, halff sleiping as I lay"—again using the motif of the dance,
the poem through the interplay of allegorical personifications gives a
criticism of the world and, more specifically, the court. The details
are worth examining.

The poem begins with the transformation of the familiar, as the dreamer's chamber appears in "ane new aray" (2), covered with paintings in "many divers hew, / Of all the nobill storyis ald and new, / Sen oure first father formed was of clay" (3–5) and "all bricht with lampis lycht" (6). This transformation is preliminary to the entry of "many lustie wicht, / Sum young, sum old, in sindry wyse arayit" (7–8). The description of this company may reflect that of the chamber and suggest that the pictures on the wall have come to life, that what follows is to be seen in the context of the "nobill storyis"—probably histories or accounts of fact detailing what are, in effect, the ways of the world.

The dominant method of the poem is one of juxtaposition and contrast. The lusty folk that enter singing, dancing, playing musical instruments, and generally making "disportis with hartis glaid and lycht" (9–10), contrast initially with the "halff sleiping" narrator. In like manner their merriment is seen to contrast with his fear, their joy with his sadness. Oppressed by Distress, Heaviness, and Langour, who appear "sad as the leid" (20) and whose song is "duilfull to heir" (23), the narrator cannot rise from his bed to join in the merriment, even though he is aided by Nobleness, Comfort, and Pleasance. After Perceiving, Discretion, and Wit analyze the situation, they see that the narrator's depression stems from his having served long in the court without reward. While Consideration helps "mantene the dance" (57), the other ladies assist the narrator in receiving "sum rewaird" in honor of "this guid new yeir" (54–55).

This first half of the poem, in the manner of the *Roman de la Rose* or a Chaucerian dream vision, functions as a way of introducing the criticism to follow. The sight of the "halff sleiping" narrator is not clear, and his insight is likewise inadequate. He does not know what is happening—"me thocht" (it seemed to me) is his customary way of introducing each new proceeding (2, 6, 11, 18, 24)—or what to make of it. The merry folk seem to him "ane guidlie companie" (13), but at the same time he fears that they may be "ane fremdlie fantasie" (14), a strange or hostile fantasy.[41] Besides lacking joy, the narrator lacks vitality; and his inability to join the dance may be seen as indicative of his sickness of spirit. Insofar as the dance functions as an aspect of music, it exists as a principle of harmony and life, specifically in accord with the celebration of "this guid new yeir"; and, significantly, the narrator is seen to be out of harmony with the holiday.

What follows, concerning the reward the dreamer should be

given for his service, is in the form of a debate between the forces of Reason, who is going to bring a new rule to the court, and those of Blind Affection, who has so far been the controlling principle at court. Dunbar now employs a different kind of allegorical personification—Sir John Kirkpaker (Churchpacker) and Sir Bet-the-kirk (Better- or Beat-the-Church)[42]—a kind seen in such late medieval visionary satires as *Piers Plowman*. More representative of a particular vicious action of man, they differ somewhat from the more general virtues and vices, and here function to challenge the claim of the narrator for preferment. Finally, with no reward immediately forthcoming, Patience counsels continuing hope.

It is this part of the poem that has led readers to classify it with Dunbar's petitions to the king, albeit as "the most unusual of these."[43] While one of Dunbar's purposes in this work is doubtless to ask for a benefice, another is to attack the greed of the clergy, the unfair ways of preferment at court, and the corrupt methods of the law courts. The poet's predicament is but one illustration of this corruption and inadequacy. In fact, the personification of Importunity—"Inoportunitie" in the manuscript (76)[44]—who says that nothing can be achieved without his help, is not presented as any kind of ideal or virtue. Besides signifying persistence, the term contained in the late fifteenth century a distinctly pejorative sense of overeagerness, unmannerliness, even troublemaking.[45] As Importunity says, he will speak "befoir the kingis face" until he either gets what he wants or deafens the king (78–79). But whatever the poet's personal or nonliterary purpose in this work, it is difficult in the light of this view of Importunity to believe that he is being importune here; most dominant is his satire of human institutions and greed.

The poem ends unexpectedly as everyone in the vision rushes out the door and shoots off a canon:

> Than as ane fary thai to duir did frak [rush],
> And schot ane gone that did so ruidlie rak [roar],
>   Quhill all the air did raird [resound] the ranebow under,
>   On Leith sandis me thocht scho brak in sounder,
> And I anon did walkin with the crak.
>
> (111–15)

The harmony—the music, dance, and pleasant disport—has changed to cacophony. Perhaps the gun's roar may function as a reflection on the argument that has been going on about preferment and the court. Or perhaps the shot is a sound from the real world, which, as such, causes everything that has appeared in the dream—dance and debate all—to be revealed in its essential unsubstantiality, as really "ane fary," a phantom. When Dunbar writes at the end that the roar was so great that "me thocht *scho*"—perhaps shot, gun, or air—broke asunder on "Leith sandis," he may be alluding to Leith, port city of Edinburgh, but also calling up the river Lethe in hell; suggesting further the demonic nature of the company that had appeared to the narrator and reinforcing his initial intuition that it was "ane fremdlie fantasie." His prayer to "Jhesu and his moder Marie" for protection (15) would seem finally to be answered.

The ending here may be compared to that in another dream vision, "This nycht, befoir the dawing cleir" (no. 4), where at the end the spirit of St. Francis, which had appeared before the poet, is seen to be a fiend: "He vaneist away with stynk and fyrie smowk; / With him me thocht all the hous end he towk,/And I awoik as wy [man] that wes in weir [doubt]" (48–50). But both the device and the point of the *Dream* seem far more complex and serious than what is detailed in the St. Francis piece. As a petition, the *Dream* is unique; as a satire, it differs from the typical catalogings of sins; as an allegorical dream vision, it is alone, going beyond the courtliness of the *Thrissil and the Rois* and the grotesquerie of the *Dance of the Sevin Deidly Synnis*. Still, to say what this poem is not is hardly sufficient, for all of its elements taken together make it one of Dunbar's most intriguing compositions.[46]

Somewhat related to this poem in its untypical blend of traditional machinery is "Amang thir freiris, within ane cloister" (no. 80).[47] In the oratory of a friary the narrator prays to God and Mary, and, thinking of Christ's passion, falls asleep. What follows for the next eleven stanzas of this unusual dream vision is a detailed account of the agony endured by Christ before and during the Crucifixion, all "for the luif" of man. The ironic contrast between Christ's act of love and man's acts of hate, traditional though it may be, is effective here; and the repeated refrain, "O mankynd, for the luif of the," functions as the poet's comment on the passion and acts to increase our awareness of the injustice.

The stanzas proceed in slow motion, as it were, beginning with Judas's betrayal (9) and working point by point up to Christ's death after "ane rude speir" is thrust into his side (90). At this point the poem alters its approach, and the next five stanzas detail the narrator's response to the agony he has been describing. Dunbar's method is again to use allegorical personifications, but, though similar in kind to those appearing in the *Dream,* these are different in effect. The others were seen as unsuccessful in their endeavors, and ultimately without point. Here, although again the narrator awakens before any explicit resolution, there is a distinct sense of purpose and hope.

The personifications Compassion, Contrition, Ruth, Remembrance, Pain, and Pity make the narrator of "Amang thir freiris" feel grief and the need to repay Christ's sacrifice. Other comparable personifications are then able to function. Grace commands the narrator to prepare a resting place for Christ (113–20). This is the narrator's soul, which through Contrition and Confession is made ready; and through Conscience, Repentance, and Penance is kept fit. With this section moving from a direct statement of the Passion to an oblique one of man's penance, the refrain changes from being an address to mankind and focuses on Christ, with a variation of the words "Thy blissit Salvatour Chryst Jesu." When the emphasis was on what happened to Christ, the refrain was directed at man; now that the stress is on man's recognition of Christ's sacrifice and of his need for repentance, the refrain refers to Christ.

In the final stanza, the poem turns away from the allegorical statement of man's preparing himself to be ready and able to receive Christ, and reveals nature as offended by the Crucifixion: "For grit terrour of Chrystis deid, / The erde did trymmill quhair I lay" (137–38). At this shock, comparable to the gunshot in the *Dream,* the narrator awakens and writes of his experience, noting in particular that this vision occurred "on Gud Fryday" (143). This dating not only makes the vision especially timely, it accounts for Dunbar's holding the Resurrection in abeyance and for his emphasizing human sin and the need for repentance. The conclusion of this poem is really found in Dunbar's celebration of the victory represented by the Resurrection, "Done is a battell on the dragon blak" (no. 81). But that is a different poem with a different theme and should not be used as a basis for examining this passion poem. Scott's criticism— that the poem is "brutal and crude," "a sado-masochistic exercise," containing "an almost Hollywoodish vulgarity and grossness of sen-

sibility"—seems to be the result of not permitting the poem to be
what it is and seems finally as wrongheaded as Pinkerton's comment
in 1786 that the poem is "as stupid as need be."[48] Even Schipper at
the end of the nineteenth century realized that Dunbar has been
successful here in raising his subject "into a somewhat higher sphere
than that of mere descriptive poetry."[49]

The subjects presented in these various satires provide proof positive of the view seen in the poem (no. 66)[50] beginning as follows:

> I seik about this warld unstabille
> To find ane sentence convenabille [fitting],
>   Bot I can nocht in all my wit
>   Sa trew ane sentence fynd off it,
> As say, it is dessaveabille.
>
> (1–5)

What begins one way, the narrator realizes, concludes all to the
contrary:

> Yisterday fair up sprang the flouris,
> This day thai ar all slane with schouris;
>   And fowllis in forrest that sang cleir,
>   Now walkis with a drery cheir,
> Full caild ar baith thair beddis and bouris.
>
> (11–15)

And this principle of mutability is taken to show the essentially
"dessaveabille" nature of the world, its state since the fall of man. As
this poem questions the validity of what seems to be, so the satires
reveal priest, courtier, craftsman, and gossip as examples of the
falseness of this world. Everything is "dessaveabille," and even the
comfort one gets from visions cannot be counted on, as is seen in the
Dream.

IV   *Prayers and Hymns*

Dunbar's moral sense, that which is the basis for both his criticism
and his instruction of man, is also the basis of his prayers to Christ
and Mary. The short and relatively simple poem known as *Ane
Orisoun* (no. 78) may provide a transition between those poems
directed at earthly inadequacy and those celebrating the faith:

Salviour, suppois my sensualitie
Subject to syn hes maid my saule of sys [often],
Sum spark of lycht and spiritualite,
Walkynnis my witt, and ressoun biddis me rys,
5   My corrupt conscience askis, clips [calls], and cryis
First grace, syn space, for to amend my mys,
Substance with honour doing none suppryis [harms],
Freyndis, prosperite, heir peax, syne hevynis blys.

In this poem, seen as Donne-like and as "comparable in conciseness
and force" to the short moralizing *Of Lyfe* (no. 76),[51] the "sensualitie" that has made the soul subject to sin is contrasted with and
seen giving way to the "spark of lycht and spiritualite" that awakens
the understanding. Although corrupt, man's conscience still begs for
grace and for a chance to make amends for its sin, to achieve in this
life prosperity and peace and afterward "hevynis blys."[52]

Whereas the "corrupt conscience" of man is the stuff of Dunbar's
satires and overt moralizings, the "hevynis blys" itself is the basis for
a few poems including at least two that are among Dunbar's finest. It
might be thought that one so critical of the world would not be
comfortable using a purely celebratory style and form, but these
religious poems may be seen as being in relation to the satires and
moralizings, much as a poem like "My prince in God, gif the guid
grace" (no. 26) is in relation to the begging poems. Although Dunbar's feet are solidly on the earth, his head is not here; he is in this
world though not of it, and his celebrations of the ideal beyond this
world ring out with a vigor, vitality, sincerity, and harmony quite
different from the bitter scorn, irony, and ambiguity that mark his
earth-directed efforts.

His poem *Of the Nativitie of Christ* (no. 79) begins with a clarion
call fitting for this other world:

Rorate celi desuper!
Hevins distill your balmy schouris,
For now is rissin the bricht day ster,
Fro the ros Mary, flour of flouris:
The cleir Sone, quhome no clud devouris,
Surminting Phebus in the est,
Is cumin of his hevinly touris;
Et nobis Puer natus est.

(1–8)

As C. S. Lewis has written, this may well be "the most lyrical of all English poems," that is, "the hardest not to sing."[53] The Latin phrases, from the liturgy for Christmas Eve and Christmas Day— derived from Isaiah 45:8 and 9:6—detailing the prophecy of the coming of Christ, not only provide the context for the English, and in the case of the last line, the refrain of the poem, they play against the English in a construct of verbal polyphony. All of creation is asked to join in the joyful song honoring Christ. The singing takes the form of related actions: sinners should be glad of the birth and do penance (17), the clergy should bow to him and do other "obser- vance devyne" (25–27), flowers should spring up "In honour of the blissit frute / That rais up fro the rose Mary" (43–44). All of heaven and earth should "be myrthfull and mak melody" and participate in the cry of "*Gloria in excelsis*" (52–53). The note of joy seen here is not, as Scott suggests, because Dunbar may at last have received his benefice;[54] rather, it is the joy that is at the heart of Dunbar's poetry, though that which is lacking in this world.

A companion piece to this Nativity hymn is *On the Resurrection of Christ* (no. 81), which has been deservedly praised as "perhaps the most powerful, certainly one of the most popular of Dunbar's poems."[55] In the same stanzaic form as the Nativity poem, though in different meter, it exhibits the same joyful music, as may be seen in its first stanza:

> Done is a battell on the dragon blak,
> Our campioun Chryst confountet hes his force;
> The yettis of hell ar brokin with a crak,
> The signe triumphall rasit is of the croce,
> The divillis trymmillis [tremble] with hiddous voce,
> The saulis ar borrowit [ransomed] and to the blis can go,
> Chryst with his blud our ransonis dois indoce [endorse]:
> *Surrexit Dominus de sepulchro.*
>
> ((1–8)

But rather than honor the new king, the poem celebrates a great victory—in Baxter's view it is "a poem of fierce joy,"[56] and for Smith it is "richer in artistic than religious seriousness."[57] Christ is the "campioun" who, in being crucified and harrowing hell, has re- deemed man from "the deidly dragon Lucifer" (9). Whereas the Nativity poem was in the imperative mood, this poem is in the indicative mood and is without the urgency of the other, although

the lines contain a "breathless rhythm" that conveys "the excite-
ment of the triumph."[58] There creation was asked to accept and
praise its new king; here the significance of what has been accomplished by the Resurrection is emphasized. Now man is not a
participant in anything; he has been the recipient of a concluded
action. In Lewis's view these two poems are related but are
"equally, but differently excellent." The Resurrection poem "is
speech rather than song, but speech of unanswerable and thunder-
ing greatness."[59]

   Whereas in the Nativity poem the stanzas were in the form of full
compound and complex sentences, the Resurrection piece uses
short sentences, most frequently one to a line, or even one to a half
line, as the entire last stanza—beginning "The fo is chasit, the battell is done ceis" (33)—indicates strikingly. These short simple sentences, far from making the poem choppy, provide a kind of incremental repetition that brings out the full significance of the Resurrection. The traditional images and phrases that fill the poem[60]
seem fresh and harmoniously blended, as each of the five stanzas is
constructed to echo the others. There is, however, something of a
progression of thought. The first stanza emphasizes the battle's
being finished and man's being released, the second stresses the
battle that has taken place against the "deidly dragon," the "crewall
serpent," the "auld kene tegir" that has lain in wait for man,
"Thinking to grip us in his clows strang" (9–13). The third stanza
continues the animal imagery, but here in reference to Christ, who
is "lyk a lamb" sacrificed and "lyk a lyone" raised up again (18–19).
Christ is also like a giant stretching aloft.[61] The animal imagery is
joined to mythological references as Christ is called Aurora, the
dawn, bursting forth radiant and bright, and "the glorius Appollo,"
the sun, gone aloft. This last image is worked out in detail as the
next stanza emphasizes how the "grit victour" is raised on high after
being wounded to the death, how "The sone that wox all paill now
schynis bricht" (27). And the final stanza returns to the imagery of
the first stanza, restating the victory and the release of man. In the
Nativity poem Christ was shown coming to the world as helpless
infant but still as king; here he leaves the world, again paradoxically,
as dead man and as victor over death.

   Related to these two celebrations of Christ is Dunbar's poem
praising the Virgin, "Hale, sterne superne! Hale, in eterne" (no.
82).[62] A *tour de force* of aureation, alliteration, and intricate rhyme,
it has been termed a poem that "glitters in its preciosity,"[63] "one of

the most artfully contrived of Scottish poems,"[64] and as near as Dunbar "ever came to 'pure' poetry."[65] Modeled on Latin hymns to Mary, the poem uses traditional images and Latinate forms as the material for a dazzling display of sounds and rhythms extended amazingly over eighty-four lines.[66] In a sense, this glorious Hail Mary is the epideictic counterpart to poems of invective such as the *Flyting*. The first stanza will serve to illustrate Dunbar's accomplishment:

> Hale, sterne superne! Hale, in eterne,
>   In Godis sicht to schyne!
> Lucerne in derne for to discerne
>   Be glory and grace devyne;
> Hodiern, modern, sempitern,
>   Angelicall regyne!
> Our tern inferne for to dispern
>   Helpe, rialest rosyne.
> *Ave Maria, gracia plena!*
>   Haile, fresche floure femynyne!
> Yerne us, guberne, virgin matern,
>   Of reuth baith rute and ryne.
>
> (1–12)[67]

Alliteration and rhyme play against each other, the Latin *Ave Maria* acts as a refrain for the seven stanzas, and the anaphoric use of "Hail," with its "l" sounds juxtaposed against the nasals that fill the stanza, punctuates the verses, giving them an urgency comparable to that seen in the Nativity piece. Again, if Dunbar was aware in his writing of the symbolic value of number—something frequently found in both Latin and English hymns to the Virgin—his using seven stanzas of twelve lines may be an intentional joining of the two numbers most suggesting, in their combination of four—number of the flesh—and three—that of the spirit—perfection and fulfillment. This blend of four and three is also continued in alternating form in the stresses of each poetic line.

Looking at the substance of Dunbar's praise, we find that he emphasizes Mary's regal qualities. Along with being "gentill nychttingale" (34) and "ros of paradys" (40), she is "hevinlie hie emprys" (38). It is this aspect that is stressed in the last two stanzas of the poem where she is "empryce of prys, imperatrice" (61); not just queen of heaven, she is, as it were, its foundation:

> Imperiall wall, place palestrall,
> Of peirles pulcritud;
> Tryumphale hall, hie trone regall
> Of Godis celsitud [greatness].
>
> (73–76)

As such she is the worthy counterpart to the glorious champion
Christ seen in Dunbar's Resurrection poem, not the humble
maiden-mother, placid rose-lily, or figure of sorrow grieving at the
foot of the cross, dominant in other Latin and vernacular lyrics.

In these three celebrations Dunbar emphasizes the joy and victory to be found in Christianity. Although he frequently presents
this world in terms of the *danse macabre* and the *memento mori*,
with the refrain *Timor mortis conturbat me* providing a major impetus for several poems, when he looks beyond man and his inadequacies, he finds only hope and wonder; and his poems change
from dirges to celebrations. Although the language in these Christian celebrations, especially in "Hale sterne superne!" may recall
the aureation and rhetorical excess seen earlier in the *Ballade of Lord
Bernard Stewart* (no. 61), here the praise and the diction seem in
order and justified. Too extreme when applied to a human being,
they here at least seem to have a subject worthy of such grandeur.

Contrasting with these celebrations and with both the satires and
moralities is "To the, O mercifull Salviour, Jesus" (no. 83).[68] Like
the *Professione di fede* once attributed to Dante, the poem gives a
comprehensive summary of medieval Christian beliefs; and like
Chaucer's *Retractation* at the end of the *Canterbury Tales,* it functions as the poet's individualized statement of the repentance he has
been urging for mankind in general. Whereas in the dream poems
the narrator is most often more acted upon than acting, here he acts
positively, repenting his sins explicitly and entirely. The first stanza
shows the directness that marks the twenty-one stanzas of this
poem:

> To the, O mercifull Salviour, Jesus,
> My King, my Lord, and my Redemar sweit,
> Befoir thy bludy figor dolorus
> I repent my synnys, with humill hairt contreit,
> That evir I did unto this hour compleit,
> Baith in werk, in word, and eik intent;
> Falling on face, full law befoir thy feit,
> I cry The mercy, and lasar to repent.
>
> (1–8)

The rest of the poem is a detailed account of what purport to be the poet's sins, organized by kind, a method that allows Dunbar to state in passing the corrective of each sin—the Seven Deeds of Corporeal Mercy, the Ten Commandments, the Articles of Truth, etc. Far from taking the confession literally,[69] we should see it as Dunbar's method of presenting the bases of Christian faith. As such, it functions as a guide for mankind and may be read, furthermore, as a definitive statement of the spiritual truths at the heart of Dunbar's poetry.

For all the ambiguity of other poems, Dunbar's entire poetic corpus may properly be read as being framed by the simple and brief prayer, "Salviour, suppois" (no. 78), and by this full-scale treatment of repentance. In this sense the poem may function as Dunbar's final statement of Truth and should be held up against the ironic ambiguities, poses, and half-truths seen by and large in his other writings. As the *Parson's Tale* functions "to knytte up" all the feast of the *Canterbury Tales* and show finally "the wey, in this viage, / Of thilke parfit glorious pilgrymage / That highte Jerusalem celestial,"[70] so this *Tabill of Confession*—no matter when written—sums up the ideals operative throughout Dunbar's writings. Without aureate diction or the machinery of dream visions or allegory, and lacking in intricate plays of sound, rhyme, rhythm, and imagery, it is still a poem that because of its content cannot be ignored by any student of Dunbar.

CHAPTER 5

The Love Poet

I Right and Wrong Loving

THE very idea of considering Dunbar as a love poet may seem incongruous in the light of what has been said of Dunbar the moralist. However, as Scott points out, "it is remarkable how many of his poems are concerned with women and sexual relations, directly and indirectly";[1] and, as will be seen, the view and treatment of love in his poetry are in accord with medieval tradition and not at all at odds with his moral positions.

"Be ye ane luvar" (no. 68)[2] has as its premise the idea that because one is a lover, he should not think he is therefore exempt from living properly: "Be ye ane luvar, think ye nocht ye suld / Be weill advysit in your governing?" (1–2). The instructions that follow are not, as has been thought, a list of the qualities necessary in a courtly lover,[3] but advice for those who would be virtuous. The refrain, "Be secreit, trew, increasing of your name," while pertinent to a lover, is also in the context provided by the three stanzas comprising the poem more than this. Not only should the lover "Be layth alway to do amis or schame" (6), he should in particular, as the entire second stanza emphasizes, be careful to speak well, not to lie, to chatter, or to jangle—admonitions that develop the "secreit" and "trew" parts of the refrain. Rather, he should be wise so that others may learn from him (21), not proud and not abashed by wicked tongues. The clear implication of the poem is in contradiction to those medieval writings showing the lover as *de facto* a man of virtue. Dunbar seems to be suggesting the opposite, that the lover must be especially concerned with his "governing" and with his good name. He should "Bewar thairwith for dreid of misdemyng" (4), not necessarily the "misdemyng" of man, but primarily that of God, as noted

98

above in the poem *Of Deming* (no. 8) and in "How sould I rewill me" (no. 9).

Love is mentioned at the beginning and end of "Be ye ane luvar" (1, 23), but nothing in between is especially pertinent to it. In fact, when Dunbar advises that the lover should "Be now and ay the maistir of your will" (13), it is doubtful that he is talking about the traditional "ideal" of earthly love, as celebrated in the stories of Tristan, Lancelot, and Troilus. In each of these works the lover is seen surrendering his will to his lady, being her servant and no longer his own master. It may be significant that the initial "Be ye ane luvar" is paralleled with the clauses, "Be ye ane lear" (9), "Be ye ane tratlar [chatterer]" (10), and "Be ye ane janglar" (11), as though all these states are variations of the same condition, or at least that such "vicis" (12) naturally accompany being a lover. Rather than being "wholly in keeping with the tradition of courtly love,"[4] at least as popularly understood, the love presented here would seem to be out of sorts with it, even as it is elsewhere presented by Dunbar.

In "My hartis tresure, and swete assured fo" (no. 50)[5] Dunbar presents a traditional courtly lover, and the excesses of emotion and language have been obvious to readers since at least the sixteenth-century Bannatyne manuscript whose colophon reads, "Quod Dumbar quhone he list to feyne,"[6] emphasizing the pretense here, though the nature of the humor is not clear. In Schipper's view, for instance, the poem is "written by one who is convinced of the utter hopelessness of his passion and has the humour to joke upon it."[7] This plea, "in ludicrously exaggerated terms,"[8] begins with a statement of how the lady's cruelty is slaying the narrator. Throughout the first five stanzas death is seen as something imminent and something synonymous with his lady love. As the first stanza states it, his love is "The finale endar of my lyfe for ever" (2). She is a "man slayar," and he asks her to stop her "slauchter" since he is her true servant and does not deserve "to go to deathe" (4–6). As the poem develops, death gets closer and closer. In the narrator's view, "My deathe chasis my lyfe so besalie / That wery is my goist to fle so fast" (15–16), the "deithe is in my breist with furious rage" (25), suggesting also the inherent relationship between earthly love and death found throughout medieval literature—it is "my deidlie passioun dolorous" (29)—until finally in the last stanza the projected death is described in detail:

In to my mynd I sall yow mercye cry,
  Quhone that my toung sall faill me to speik,
And quhill that nature me my sycht deny,
  And quhill my ene [eyes] for pane incluse and steik [shut],
  And quhill the dethe my hart in sowndir breik,
And quhill my mynd may think and towng may steir;
And syne [then], fair weill, my hartis Ladie deir!

(43–49)

But there is a problem with the meaning of this stanza. According to Scott, the passage suggests the continuation of the narrator's love: "Even when his tongue fails to speak, being worn out, he will still importune her for mercy in his mind, and when death eventually overtakes him, he will wish her well."[9] For Ridley, on the other hand, who rightly points out "quhill" should be taken as meaning "until," the last stanza gives "an adroit turn . . . to make glaringly clear the unreality of the poem's exaggeration."[10] But the particular meaning of the passage needs to be clarified. The narrator says, in effect, that after he is unable to speak, he will continue to ask for mercy in his mind, even to the time that he loses his sight, and until his heart is broken apart. But then, in the penultimate line, there seems to occur a change of pace. It is as though after this death— perhaps a projection of the living death represented by love—his "mynd may think and towng may steir" (48), as they have not been able to do since love overcame them. Freed of love, then ("syne") the lover can once again think and speak clearly and can finally say farewell to his lady: "fair weill, my hartis Ladie deir!" While on one level "deir" means beloved or precious, on another level it may mean harmful or deadly.[11] Taken this way, "Ladie" may then make sense as a play on "loathe"—"lath" or "lad" in Middle Scots— meaning hateful or displeasing,[12] and represent the narrator's final evaluation of his love. Even without this paronomasia, the poem gives more than a picture of excessive love; as a study in irony it offers a reevaluation of this love.

In the light of this poem and such pieces, we may best arrive at an understanding of "Sweit rois of vertew and of gentilnes" (no. 49),[13] which may be quoted in its entirety:

Sweit rois of vertew and of gentilnes,
Delytsum lyllie of everie lustynes,
  Richest in bontie and in bewtie cleir,

And everie vertew that is held most deir,
5   Except onlie that ye ar mercyles.

In to your garthe this day I did persew,
Thair saw I flowris that fresche wer of hew;
    Baith quhyte and reid moist lusty wer to seyne,
    And halsum herbis upone stalkis grene;
10   Yit leif nor flour fynd could I nane of rew.

I dout that Merche, with his caild blastis keyne,
Hes slane this gentill herbe that I of mene,
    Quhois petewous deithe dois to my hart sic pane
    That I wald mak to plant his rute agane.
15   So confortand his levis unto me bene.

It has been conjectured that the "ladye" of the poem is Mistress
Musgrave, referred to in the *Dance in the Quenis Chalmer*,[14] or
even "the Queen herself."[15] When not attempting to identify the
lady, the critic may still feel that the poem is, as Scott puts it, "a
simple complaint, in the romantic style, of his lady's cruelty."[16]

Whereas the image of rose and lily is traditionally found in praises
of the Virgin Mary, and in these the dominant quality cited is usually mercy, in Dunbar's poem the object of the poet's love is, ironically, "mercyles" (5). Also here the traditional significations of the
two flowers are reversed: lily would be more appropriately associated with virtue and rose with lustiness (1–2). In Speirs' view
this reversing may be designed to emphasize the interchanging
qualities and suggest that "the lady is virtuous and desirable at the
same time."[17] But the reversing may also be a way of ironically using
the conventional associations. In the context of the first stanza—
with its emphasis on "vertew," "gentilnes," "bontie," and "bewtie"—the lack of mercy is especially noticeable and tends to under-
cut the other qualities. That is, the lady personified here in terms of
flowers may be seen functioning as a parody of the ideal love that has
mercy, or grace, as its end.

Even though in the lady's garden there are many flowers, "Baith
quhyte and reid" (8)—the colors of earthly love as well as of lily and
rose—and "halsum herbis" (9), because of the lack of "rew" all of
these appear to be inadequate. The remainder of the poem plays on
the meanings of "rew" as herb and as "pity"—what is "so confortand" to the narrator (15). The special irony here is that, as cited in

medieval herbals, rue (*ruta graveolens*) was especially effective in counteracting lust: it "wasteth the humour of Venus, and abateth in males the appetite of Venus." Again: "it is properly given against the seruice of Venus, and to them that dreameth of lecherye."[18] As a corrective to amorous desire, it is ironically included in the garden of love described in the poem.

This lyric, elegant and subtle, combining understatement and wit, may very well be "Dunbar's most perfect lyric," its "pure singing" perhaps reflecting an actual tune.[19] But it is also essentially ironic in its presentation of love, which is comparable to that found in "My hartis tresure, and swete assured fo" (no. 50), even to the parallel play on death. Although it is without the overstatement and exaggeration of this other poem, its tone should not cause its real parodic elements, which would surely have been apparent to Dunbar's audience, to be missed.

II   *Allegories of Love*

Initially similar in tone and in details to "Sweit rois of vertew" is the allegory known as *Bewty and the Presoneir* (no. 54),[20] which begins as follows:

> Sen that I am a presoneir
> Till hir that farest is and best,
> I me commend, fra yeir till yeir,
> In till hir bandoun [dominion] for to rest.
> I govit [gazed] on that gudliest,
> So lang to luk I tuk laiseir,
> Quhill I wes tane withouttin test,
> And led furth as a presoneir.
>
> (1–8)

The arrangement of events here is unusual. The first quatrain states the condition of the narrator—that he is "a presoneir" of love and that he intends to remain in his lady's dominion. The second quatrain states in effect how he became a prisoner, that by gazing so long at his lady he was taken willingly.

In the second stanza the allegory develops as the speaker shows himself so wounded by her sweet demeanor and fresh beauty that he willingly goes to "the castell of pennance" owned by Beauty; and because of his "luking," he becomes, as Beauty says, "my ladeis presoneir" (16). From this point the poem is marked by so much ambiguity and confusion of details that these complexities could hardly be other than purposeful. For instance, even though the narrator becomes prisoner of Beauty's lady, he is later seen as prisoner of Beauty herself (104, 112) and as "Luvis presoneir" (96). While this mixing of detail may perhaps be explained by the nature of the allegory, other confusions are not so easily removed. Such may be seen in the third stanza:

> Thai had me bundin to the yet,
> Quhair Strangenes had bene portar ay,
> And in deliverit me thairat,
> And in thir termis can thai say,
> "Do wait [keep watch], and lat him nocht away;"
> Quo Strangenes unto the porteir,
> "Ontill my lady, I dar lay,
> Ye be to pure a presoneir."

$$(17-24)$$

The "thai" must be Beauty's ladies, but the porter seems first to be Strangenes, that is, offishness or reserve, then someone addressed by Strangenes, then the prisoner himself. Few critics have commented on this ambiguity, although it may be such details as these that led to Schipper's view that the poem was "composed in a spirit of playful humour."[21] Scott's conclusion that the ambiguity is the result of Dunbar's heart's not really being in the poem—if indeed it is by him at all[22]—begs the question. The mix-up continues as the narrator, cast in a deep dungeon and fettered without lock or chain, is criticized as not worthy of being a prisoner. Strangenes says he is "to pure [poor] a presoneir" (24), and Scorn accuses him of being "to townage"—that is, too townish or uncourtly—to be "my ladeis presoneir" (39–40). Moreover, the dream and waking worlds are confused in the course of the poem. Although there has been no mention of the narrator's dreaming all this, after Good Hope whispers to him to write a letter to his lady asking for pity, he "wouk" and did so.

The poem then becomes the account of a battle, as the forces of Pity, led by Lust, besiege the castle in an attempt to release the prisoner. And again matters are confused. In response to the attack, Comparison[23] says to the attackers "Ye will nocht wyn the presoneir" (64). In the next stanza in response to the destruction of one of the castle's towers Comparison appears quite differently:

> Comparisone began to lour,
> And cryit furth, "I yow requeir [ask],
> Soft and fair and do favour,
> And tak to yow the presoneir."
>
> (69–72)

Although the "lour" or scowl does not seem to be in accord with the "soft and fair" words, the meaning would seem to be that Comparison says he will surrender the prisoner. But in the next stanzas, the gates to the castle are set afire by the attackers, Strangenes is burned to death (75–76), Scorn has a skewer put through his nose, Comparison is buried alive, Langour leaps from the castle and breaks his neck, and Good Fame is drowned in a sack (81–87).

With the release of the prisoner the poem is still not concluded, for Slander raises an army against Lust, and Envy abuses "Luvis presoneir" (96). Then Matrimony drives Slander "to the west se cost" (100)—perhaps, as Scott suggests, to where the Gaelic Scots reside[24]—and endorses a bond of friendship between "Bewty and the presoneir" (103–4). The final stanza shows the heir of Good Fame receiving from Matrimony his inheritance and living still, "as it wes resone, / With Bewty and the presoneir" (111–12). To say that this "allegory of courtly love" is "unexceptional save for the innovation of Matrimony's putting all to rights"[25] is hardly to face its unusualness. As much in the morality tradition seen, for instance, in the Middle Scots *King Hart,* formerly attributed to Douglas, as in the love-allegory tradition stemming from the *Roman de la Rose,* the poem is an interesting blend of the real and the fanciful. Into the courtly never-never land of make believe comes real violence. It is as though Dunbar has reversed matters so that instead of seeing the human by means of the allegorical, the allegorical appears in terms of the human.

The confusions of who's who and what's what ultimately give a reflection of love's essential nature. The "happy" ending here is not without ambiguity, and the movement of the poem in effect returns to the opening lines, indicating that after all the fighting and killing, after the supposed release of the prisoner, he is still in his state of voluntary and perpetual bondage. The term "presoneir," found in the first line, becomes the key refrain word of each stanza, in its repetition demonstrating that this is the constant and continuing condition of a lover. While clearly a study in prosody, and perhaps a "counterpart in verse of a court pageant,"[26] the poem is also an ironic picture of love and one that is diametrically opposed to the conditions detailed in "Be ye ane luvar" (no. 68).

More in the tradition of the *Roman de la Rose* is the *Goldyn Targe* (no. 56),[27] a work that has been called, on the one hand, Dunbar's "supreme performance in the aureate style"[28] and, on the other, "a monument to the fact that a poem cannot be made out of an interest purely in language, and the manipulation and arrangement of it."[29] No matter that modern taste is not especially attracted to such poetry, in Dunbar's time the achievement of the *Goldyn Targe* was especially valued. Not only was the poem included in the Chepman and Myllar printing, as one of six by the poet, Lindsay, in the *Testament of the Papyngo*, praises "Dunbar, quhilk language had at large / As maye be sene in tyll his golden targe."[30]

The poem cannot really be classified as an allegory. As C. S. Lewis realizes, "Its simple allegory (that the poet is temporarily defended from love by reason) is little more than a peg, but an adequate peg, on which to hang its poetry".[31] Denton Fox, in a good analysis of the poem, affirms that in fact it does not depend on "maintaining a clear allegorical narrative."[32] It is little concerned with narrative—it avoids using any dialogue at all, thus reducing the entire battle between the forces of Love and Reason "to the simplicity of a dumb show"; it lacks "any real interior monologue," thus decreasing "the human and psychological elements" in the work.[33] If anything, the poem is a construct of literary language in which, so it would seem, Dunbar puts as many obstacles in his path as he can, so as to show how he can overcome or get beyond them. His stanzaic form, for instance, originally invented by Chaucer in his unfinished *Anelida and Arcite*, is extremely demanding—iambic pentameter rhyming *a a b a a b b a b*, thus using two rhymes in each nine-line stanza—and has been used in only one other major poem, Douglas's *Palace of Honour*. Although it might be too much to suggest, as Fox does, that the *Goldyn Targe* is "a poem about poetry," it is clearly a verbal creation in which language is pushed to its extremes of splendor.[34]

The first part of the poem, stanzas 1–5, represents most fully the work of the poet *in imitatio* of God the creator of nature. Here the creation of natural beauty is through language, the special gift of God to man. Not that the poet is copying nature, or recreating in words its beauties as a rival to the work of God, or attempting, in the

manner of neoclassical writers, to refine nature. Rather, he is celebrating creation by seeing beyond its surface and recognizing the
special thing it is. In Fox's view, the *Goldyn Targe* is "an exception-
ally flat and two-dimensional poem," making "no pretense of being
rounded and lifelike, or, on the other hand, of containing any complexities of thought."[35] Again, "Dunbar devotes his very considera-
ble poetic energies to fitting words into a meticulously interlocked
pattern and creating a hard and beautiful surface as substantial and
as self-suficient as a piece of enamelwork."[36] Although this description might not do justice to the rich luxuriance Dunbar creates in
the first part of the poem, in terms of the views Fox is countering,
he is absolutely right, and his critical perception valuable. What Fox
does not recognize, beyond this, is that the "beautiful surface" is not
of the ordinary world of nature. Dunbar looks within nature to its
essence and celebrates this as though it were the surface. The result
is a series of stanzas that seem less allegorical than visionary, even
approaching the mystical in their splendor.

The dawn and spring created by the poet in the opening stanzas,
as he describes the rose garden ("rosere") are not designed to call up
a prelapsarian world; rather, they are of a new idealized, purified
world, one in which it is not at all odd for the coming of dawn to be
described in aureate terms as "Up sprang the goldyn candill
matutyne [morning], / With clere depurit [purified] bemes cristal-
lyne" (4–5). Similarly, the landscape can be graphically referred to
in obviously artificial terms: "Anamalit was the felde wyth all col-
ouris, / The perly droppis schake in silvir schouris, / Quhill all in
balme did branch and levis flete" (13–15). What is created is a world
combining heaven and earth, one showing nature in idealized,
purified, and rarified splendor:"The skyes rang for schoutyng of the
larkis, / The purpur hevyn, our scailit in silvir sloppis [bands], /
Ourgilt the treis, branchis, lef, and barkis" (25–27). Such cohesion
results in a transformation of the norm, a going beyond the usual
surface to that ideal pattern reflected by it. But such clarity of vision
can hardly be sustained, and it is no wonder that the poet falls
asleep.

In the "dremes fantasy" (49) that follows, the human world is
presented as an extension of, and in the same manner as, the splendid natural world. This human world is really one of allegorical
personifications, and is to the actual world of man as the earlier
projection of idealized nature is to actual nature. At the same time,

the world of man is described in the same terms used for the idealized setting. For instance, the sail that appears in the east—"agayn the orient sky" (50)—is described as part of nature, "als quhite as blossum upon spray" and "brycht as the stern of day" (51–52). The ladies that land are "Als fresch as flouris that in May up spredis, / In kirtillis grene" (59–60). With their coming, "all the feldis wyth thai lilies quhite / Depaynt war brycht" (65–66). Created is a "paradise complete" (72), full of all the gods and goddesses especially pertinent to nature and love, everyone arrayed in green, playing, singing, and dancing.

Within the third part of the poem, beginning with line 127, the pageant comes to life, as it were, as the forces of Love assault the dreamer. Although he is defended for a time by Reason, "that nobil chevallere" (153), the forces of Love prevail. Reason is blinded and banished, and the narrator taken prisoner:

> Than was I woundit to the deth wele nere,
> And yoldyn as a wofull prisonnere
>   To lady Beautee, in a moment space;
> Me thoucht scho semyt lustiar of chere,
> Efter that Resoun tynt [lost] had his eyne clere,
>   Than of before, and lufliare of face:
> Quhy was thou blyndit, Resoun? quhi, allace!
> And gert [caused] ane hell my paradise appere,
>   And mercy seme, quhare that I fand no grace.
>
> (208–16)

The narrator is next misled by Dissimulation, smiled upon by Fair Calling, "fed wyth wordis fair" by Cherishing (219), embraced and favored "a quhile" by New Acquaintance (220); but then his fortunes turn, and Daunger takes him to Heaviness, where he must remain.

In contrast to what is seen in *Bewty and the Presoneir* love is not something finally attractive or even redeemable, and the transition from falling in love to losing love takes only twelve lines. The ending here is quite different from that of the other allegory. Eolus, "Lord of Windis," blows his "bugill" (229–30)—doubtless an echo of the trumpet Sklaundre blown by Eolus in Chaucer's *House of Fame*—and the beautiful dream world is destroyed:

> with the blast the levis all to-schuke;
> And sudaynly, in the space of a luke,

All was hyne [hence] went, thare was bot wildernes,
Thare was no more bot birdis, bank, and bruke.

(231–34)

Beautiful as this world has seemed with its gods and goddesses and allegorical figures, it is shown finally to be ephemeral and unreal. As everyone leaves in the ships, they fire guns, "Till that the reke [smoke] raise to the firmament, / The rochis all resownyt wyth the rak [noise], / For rede [fear] it semyt that the raynbow brak" (239–41). And at this the dreamer awakens, no longer Beauty's prisoner. But this account of love is only one part, and not the main one, of the *Goldyn Targe*. Insofar as the poem does speak of love, however, it is clearly critical, showing that passion can affect one only after Reason has been overcome, and that it will necessarily lead to "Hevynesse."

The climax here, with the shooting of the guns, is like that of the *Dream* (no. 60), although there the poet's awakening concludes the poem, In the *Goldyn Targe*, however, when the dreamer awakens and hears "the joyfull birdis" singing "merily" (245), the poem continues. But what world he is in is not clear:

Suete war the vapouris, soft the morowing,
Halesum the vale, depaynt wyth flouris ying;
    The air attemperit, sobir, and amene [mild];
    In quhite and rede was all the felde besene,
Throu Naturis nobil fresch anamalyng,
    In mirthfull May, of eviry moneth Quene.

(247–52)

Although Scott interprets this awakening as a return to this world,[37] the language of the passage, as well as the description of nature, recalls the aureate diction and splendor of the first part when the poet describes the rose garden. And the "anamalyng" done there seems to be continued here. From dream of love, and the nightmare world it brings, the poet returns to an ideal setting of natural love. The movement may be understood as one from Venus to Nature— like that seen in Chaucer's *Parliament of Fowls*—but we see no return to the "actual" ordinary world.

At the end Dunbar presents his work in the tradition of Chaucer, Gower, and Lydgate, the triumverate standing for the beginning of artful writing in English. Chaucer's "fresch anamalit termes celicall [heavenly]" (257) may be related to "Naturis nobil fresch anamalyng" (251), and the language he produced is that "surmounting eviry tong terrestriall" (260), as much as the natural world in this poem surmounts the ordinary world, that which "Oure rude langage has clere illumynate, / And faire ourgilt oure speche, that imperfyte / Stude" (266–68). Indeed, the *Goldyn Targe* is finally about poetry in the sense that it is a presentation or celebration of what the poet can achieve. Before the development of poetry in the writings of Chaucer, "This Ile before was bare and desolate / Off rethorike or lusty fresch endyte" (269–70). In this poem Dunbar has made his attempt to add to the enameling, though he fears that his effort is inadequate: "Rude is thy wede, disteynit, bare, and rent, / Wele aucht thou be aferit of the licht" (278–79).[38] And it is on this strangely apologetic note that the poem ends.

Related to *Bewty and the Presoneir* and the *Goldyn Targe* as allegory is the *Thrissil and the Rois* (no. 55), but this poem is properly a celebration of a particular marriage, not a piece detailing the workings of love or marriage. Still, one section in particular is pertinent to a discussion of the *Goldyn Targe*. Nature commands the gods Neptune and Eolus not to disturb the world on the wedding day:

> Dame Nature gaif ane inhibitioun thair
> To fers Neptunus, and Eolus the bawld,
> Nocht to perturb the wattir nor the air,
> And that no schouris, nor blastis cawld,
> Effray suld flouris nor fowlis on the fold.
>
> (64–68)

Apparently it is easy for the world of love to be disturbed, and this is precisely what happens when Eolus blows his "bugill" at the end of the *Goldyn Targe*.

That matrimony is no necessary assurance of happiness in love or of continuing love is the theme of "Quha will behald of luve the chance" (no. 51),[39] "chance" meaning varying course. The point is that because love has a "sueit dissavyng countenance" and "fair dissimulance," one cannot count on it (2–4). Marked from the beginning by "inconstance" and "variance," it does not hold with "continuance" (5–7). Its "schort plesance" will not last (11). Using only two rhymes for twenty-four lines, the poet drives home the point of love's essential mutability. To ask love to be anything other than mutable, insist the final lines, is like asking a dead man to dance (21–24). This image is probably not gratuitous, for the varying course of love leads only to "care [sorrow]" (16) and finally to death. Matrimony is no solution here.

III   *Dialogues of Love*

As Dunbar could write elegantly and obliquely about the state of love, so he could write amusedly and directly about lovemaking. In "This hindir nycht in Dumfermeling" (no. 27) he uses the form of a fable showing a fox seducing a lamb. The situation is different from what is usual in fables, like Henryson's, as well as different from the treatment of sex in Chaucer's *Nun's Priest's Tale*. It is not just that presenting animals as lovers is necessarily humorous; it is also that Dunbar creates an incongruity like that seen in Chaucer's *Merchant's Tale* in the picture of January and May in bed. The humor comes from the poet's use of incongruous language—as when the fox asks for grace while the lamb calls on the Virgin for help (12–13), or when the fox swears "be God / That he suld nocht tuich hir prenecod [pincushion]" (39)—and from Dunbar's never allowing us to forget the mismatch—"The silly lame wes all to small / To sic ane tribbill to hald ane bace" (18–19), and when the fox embraces her, he "wald haif riddin hir lyk ane rame" (6). At the same time, throughout the poem is a sense that the sexual activity is ultimately a euphemism for the more "natural" act of the fox, his killing and devouring the lamb: "Scho wes ane morsall of delyte; / He lovit na yowis auld, tuch, and sklender" (23–24). And as he embraces and kisses her, dominant are "His girnand gamis," his grimacing gums (34). To all of this the narrator responds with the refrain, "And that me thocht ane ferly cace," a wondrous thing. Regardless of the possibility that the poem may be a playful recounting of one of James IV's amorous escapades, it still exists mainly as the kind of adventure detailed in fabliau literature.

What is incongruity in "This hindir nycht in Dumfermeling" is largely tomfoolery in "In secreit place this hyndir nycht" (no. 28),[40] as terms of endearment are burlesqued and used as a means of detailing the lovemaking. As the previous poem put love literally on an animal level, so this piece—in the same stanzaic form—reduces the courtly language of love to baby talk and apparent nonsense. After the first two lines, where the poet states that he overheard what follows, the voices of the lovers take over the poem. Such alternating dialogue of love is a commonplace in medieval literature, appearing in the form of the comic pastoral in Henryson's *Robene and Makene*. The pastoral element is pertinent in Dunbar's poem, for although the "secreit place" is not described, the dominant imagery is taken from nature. The first stanza shows the undercutting of courtly language as the "beyrne" says to his "bricht," "My huny, my hart, my hoip, my heill, / I have bene lang your luifar leill" (2–4). While none of these terms of endearment is in itself odd or even amusing, the alliterative heaping-up initiates the wordplay that continues into the rest of the poem.

Aside from anatomical references, the affectionate terms come mainly from animal and plant names and are frequently presented in terms of food. Most attention in the imagery is paid to the belly, the "wambe" that is full of love (18). The "beyrne" is described as a "belly huddrun" (38), a term implying glutton, as well, perhaps, as that which causes the belly to be full. Also bovine imagery—"calfe" (23), "stirk [ox]" (54)[41]—and hircine imagery—"kyd" and perhaps "capirculyoun" (43)[42]—are emphasized here. Sexual and gastronomic images seem to be purposefully confused. He is her "unspaynit gyane" (unweaned giant), with "moderis mylk" still in his "mychane" (36–37). If "mychane" means "machine," in effect, phallus, the milk may be a euphemism, as well as an unexpected gastronomic image. Similarly, he is her "chirrie" (52), though his beard is spattered with "cale" (9). She is "sweit as the hunye" (15)[43] and his "sweit possodie" (30), perhaps sheepshead broth, but also perhaps another sexual euphemism.

The flower references in the poem are likewise confused. She is a "claver" and a "curldodie" (29),[44] as well as a "huny soppis" (30), meaning honeysuckle and being perhaps another sexual reference. His phallus is a "quhillelillie" (34), apparently a play on the shape of the lily, as well as one, ironically, on the flower's traditional association with purity. At the end of the poem, when he gives to her "ane apill rubye" (57), his offering is not only a parody of the courtly gift, a ruby ring, ruby being the gem symbolizing love,[45] but it may be calling up the fall of man with its change from a state of innocence to one of sexuality. It is after this exchange of apple that the two lovers begin to play the "dery dan" (60), another, and in this case obvious, euphemism.

Most noticeable in this poem are the occurrences of reduplication. She refers to him as "My belly huddrun, my swete hurle bawsy, / My huny gukkis, my slawsy gawsy" (38–39). He in turn responds with "My tendir gyrle, my wallie gowdye, / My tyrlie myrlie, my crowdie mowdie" (45–46).[46] While these terms cannot be explained away as gibberish, sound would seem to be more important here than meaning, and the reduplication influences sound more than it does sense. The poem may be viewed as joining the *Flyting* and "Complane I wald" (no. 19), with their use of invective, and "Hale, sterne superne" (no. 82), with its intricate language of praise, as one of Dunbar's linguistic *tours de force*. As a love poem, "In secreit place" shows courtship and lovemaking in their humorous essence. And the courtly lover, for all his fine words, is no more noble than the speaker here.

One other love poem, "In May as that Aurora did upspring" (no. 63),[47] puts fable, aureate language, and allegory in the form of a debate between a merle and a nightingale. But the poem is unlike "In secreit place" in that it concerns the nature of right-loving. It is also different from such an allegory as the *Goldyn Targe*, and in presenting a definitive statement of the ideal of love that is at the foundation of all Dunbar's poetry, it may be seen as most like the moralities. Ultimately, in spite of all its trappings resembling those of ostensibly secular verse, it is, as Scott realizes, a religious poem.[48]

Debate about love is within a tradition going back in English to the twelfth-century *Owl and the Nightingale*, and continuing in later Middle English to Lydgate's *Churl and the Bird* and the *Thrush and the Nightingale*, where, as in this poem, one side is clearly the victor. The debate here contains two views of love, one, that of the merle, or blackbird, advocating an immersion in worldly love—"This wes hir sentens sueit and delectable, / A lusty lyfe in luves service bene" (7–8), the last line being her refrain. Against this position is the nightingale, whose "sentens trew" is that "all luve is lost bot upone God allone" (15–16), the last line being the nightingale's refrain. The merle's position functions as a celebration of the creation, and she begins with a call for "ye luvaris" to join nature participating in love:

"Awalk, ye luvaris, O, this May.
Lo, fresche Flora hes flurest every spray,
As natur hes hir taucht, the noble quene,

> The feild bene clothit in a new array;
> A lusty lyfe in luvis service bene."
>
> (20–24)

Opposed to this is the nightingale's criticism that the merle's words lack "gud sentens"—"For boith is tynt [lost] the tyme and the travaill / Of every luve bot upone God allone" (30–32)—in that they do not recognize that in this world mutability is the norm. No matter how beautiful things seem, it is but a surface beauty, one "enameled," as it were, that will of necessity be lost. The "new array" of Nature (23) presented here by the merle may thus be related to what was seen at the beginning of the *Goldyn Targe*, and it functions to help us understand that this world cannot last.

The merle, as celebrant of "the law of kynd" (37), affirms that "yewth" and "crukit aige" (38) are necessarily opposed, and that the holiness pertinent to old age is grotesque when found in youth—"Of yung sanctis growis auld feyndis but faill" (35). The nightingale acts to syncretize all of creation and all ages—"both in yewth and eild, and every hour, / The luve of God most deir to man suld be" (42–43)—and to suggest that love of God is the principle governing all love in the world of nature. The beauty of women, continues the nightingale, answering further objections of the merle, exists not for the purpose of causing them to be loved but so that God their creator should be praised. Not only for creating such beauty as that of women, but for "every gudnes that bene to cum or gone, / The thank redoundis to him in every place" (62–63). Man should not think that all love is necessarily based on charity and therefore good; it is easy for him to "tak in his lady sic delyt" (74) that he forgets her creator. Her white "cullour" might seem to him his heaven, and her golden hair be apt to blind him to "lufe that is perfyt" (76–79).

The final argument of the merle is a cataloging, in the manner of courtly love poems, of the good that can come to man from love:

> "Lufe is caus of honour ay,
> Luve makis cowardis manheid to purchas,
> Luve makis knychtis hardy at assey,
> Luve makis wrechis full of lergenes [generosity],
> Luve makis sueir [slothful] folkis full of bissines,
> Luve makis sluggirdis fresche and weill besene,
> Luve changis vyce in vertewis nobilnes."
>
> (81–87)

The nightingale's refutation is simple and concise: "Trew is the contrary" (89). Worldly love "blindis men" (90) and makes them drunk and unable to use their wits: "of wo thai ar nocht war, / Quhill that all wirchip away be fro thame gone, / Fame, guddis, and strenth" (93–95). At this point the merle confesses her error: worldly love is "bot vanite" and will bring man "in the feindis net." The opposite is to "luve the luve that did for his lufe de" (97–103), and the poem concludes with the two birds singing a duet advising man to love God "that hes the wrocht" (106) and that "with his deid the bocht" (111). This song makes the narrator's "thochtis grene" (115). No matter whether sleeping or walking, he is comforted by knowing that "all lufe is lost bot upone God allone" (120).

This view is that not only of Dunbar the cleric but of Dunbar the poet,[49] and it should be seen as the corrective for all the wrong loving—of world and of man—detailed throughout his poetry. The view is reinforced by a poem in the form of a contrast between the two loves by one who has experienced both, "Now culit is Dame Venus brand" (no. 52).[50] There is absolutely no evidence for thinking that the poem refers to a particular love of the poet,[51] or that it reflects "the story of his tormented love" that is "everywhere manifest" in his poetry and that underlies his "spiritual struggles,"[52] or that it, along with the piece about the merle and the nightingale, was written for the "moral comfort" of the queen after James was killed at Flodden.[53] As "a farewell to physical and praise of spiritual love,"[54] the poem is in a long tradition, with counterparts throughout medieval literature. The first two stanzas—the best in the poem—state the theme very well:

> Now culit is Dame Venus brand;
> Trew luvis fyre is ay kindilland,
> And I begyn to undirstand,
> In feynit luve quhat foly bene;
> Now cumis aige quhair yewth hes bene,
> And trew luve rysis fro the splene.
>
> Quhill Venus fyre be deid and cauld,
> Trew luvis fyre nevir birnis bauld;
> So as the ta [one] lufe waxis auld,
> The tothir dois incres moir kene:
> Now cumis aige quhair yewth hes bene,
> And trew lufe rysis fro the splene.

(1–12)

The spleen, supposed seat of the affections,[55] finally, as it were, releases "trew luve"; for this "lufe perfyte" cannot exist while one delights in "fenyeit lufe" (14–15).

Although the theme is clear from the outset, the poem goes beyond making this point. Its fifteen stanzas may be divided in thirds. The first five stanzas state the point. The second group of five (31–60) relate in effect the narrator's conclusions based on personal experience at "luvis court" (26), where for one joy there were fifteen troubles. The "dreid" that had formerly marked him has now changed to "confort" (31–32), "diseis" to "eis" (38–39). Now he is freed from "jelosy" (43) and "schame" (49), for, as the third part of the poem details (61–90), he has a new love, Christ, who acts as a manifestation of the "trew luve" referred to in the refrain:

> Ane lufe so fare, so gud, so sueit,
> So riche, so rewthfull, and discreit,
> And for the kynd of man so meit,
> Nevir moir salbe nor yet hes bene.
>
> (73–76)

His final advice is that one may with "grace of God" recognize in youth "This fals dissavand warldis blis" that "gydis man in flouris grene" (85–88). Again, not only love but the attractions of the created world, the "flouris grene" in particular and the "warldis blis" in general, may cause man to do "foly" and to prefer the creation to the Creator.

IV   *In Praise of Women*

Related to Dunbar's view of love is his attitude toward women. Sometimes, as in the *Twa Cummeris* (no. 46), women are used to symbolize the pleasures of this world and the vices of gluttony and lechery. Sometimes their sexual natures are especially singled out, as in "Thir ladyis fair, That makis repair" (no. 48) and in "Madam, your men said thai wald ryd" (no. 31). Opposed to this view would seem to be "Now of wemen this I say for me" (no. 45).[56] Because of its eulogy of women this piece has been seen as untypical of Dunbar, and his authorship of it has been questioned, though both Bannatyne and Maitland assign the poem to him.[57] Schipper's criticism that the poem is Dunbar's apology "for former offences committed against the fair sex,"[58] seems to miss the point, as does

Scott's analysis that the poem "seems to have been written for an audience of women and is a blatant piece of flattery."[59]

Instead of "sincere praise," the poem more likely expresses "a heavy-handed irony"[60] in which one side of the traditional medieval view of women is presented as the entire view. At one and the same time women were seen as descended from Eve, whose sin, especially her lack of obedience, was responsible for man's fall from Paradise, and from Mary, chaste mother of Christ who in effect countered Eve's sin. In "Now of wemen," however, Dunbar seems to have taken the Marian redemption and applied it literally to all women. The opening lines make this point clear:

> Now of wemen this I say for me,
> Off erthly thingis nane may bettir be;
> Thay suld haif wirschep and grit honoring
> Off men, aboif all uthir erthly thing.
>
> (1–4)

The "for me" (1) may suggest that the narrator is giving individual opinion, not universal truth. Praise of "erthly thingis" is hardly what the veneration of Mary is about. And woman as earthly, physical being is what is dominant in this poem. There is no projected transformation from flesh to spirit; in fact, in a rather strange couplet, Dunbar writes, "Sen that of wemen cumin all ar we, / Wemen ar wemen and sa will end and de" (7–8). Although the association of women with death is clear here, little else is; and as the lines stand, they do not really make sense. What Dunbar may have written, however, is that "since we are all come from women, then it is to be understood that 'we men ar wemen' and so will end and die." This Donne-like twist may continue in a play on the sexual connotations of "de" at the end of the line and suggest the role of sex in the fall of man. When Dunbar goes on in the next line to curse the fruit that "wald put the tre to nocht" (9), he seems to be not only talking about man's criticism of his mother, but alluding to the fruit that caused man to lose the Tree of Life. The proverbial maxims in this poem are at best half-truths and should not be confused with wisdom.

To say that women "suld haif wirschep and grit honoring" (3) is to give to them what belongs only to the Virgin. Although mankind may worship Mary, mother of God and mediatrix for sinners, women do not automatically partake of this worship. Dunbar, however, ironically states the opposite: since Mary bore Christ, who is source of all goodness, then "all wemen of us suld haif honoring, / Service and luve, aboif all uthir thing" (33–34). Earlier the phrase was "erthly thing." To think that such lines—these are the final ones in the poem—could be designed to be taken at face value is to forget that the author of these lines was a cleric and to misunderstand the medieval view of things of this world. In the *Thrush and the Nightingale*, the Middle English debate about the worth of women, after all the arguments for and against women, the climaxing one is that if women were all bad, Christ would never have been born of one. But in Dunbar's poem no criticism of women appears. In fact, the narrator says such should never be uttered. Anyone speaking of any lack in women is "without intelligence" (26)—"Exylit he suld be of all gud cumpany" (24).

The poem may finally be read as comparable to Chaucer's "praise" of women in the *Legend of Good Women* and to the fifteenth-century *Praise of Women* once attributed to Chaucer and included in the Bannatyne manuscript. The all-virtuous woman is not to be found in this world—the point of Chaucer's Clerk in his tale of Griselda—and Dunbar the cleric knew this full well. The ironic praise given in "Now of wemen" may also be compared to that in Dunbar's "Sweit rois of vertew" (no. 49), although there the subject was a particular woman, not womankind.

This praise may also be related to that given in the *Tretis of the Tua Mariit Wemen and the Wedo* (no. 47).[61] The women overheard by the narrator are described in terms that would suggest them to be splendid creatures, paragons of beauty and nobility. But by the time they speak, revealing their thoughts on marriage, they are seen to be the opposite of what they appear, resembling finally the speakers in the *Twa Cummeris* more than fine ladies. The poem employs a mixture of high and low styles and subject matter. Whereas the resulting "highly effective contrast between the aureate style, the beauty of surroundings and speakers and the grossness of their sentiments has been discussed at length,"[62] readers are still in disagreement about Dunbar's point. Baxter, for instance, questions whether the poem can really be called a satire, for, in his view, "the poet is indifferent to the moral aspects. It is a distortion of the poem to claim that Dunbar represents the ladies as objects of infamy."[63] Speirs sees in the *Tretis* a poem where Dunbar's "comic zest," his "sheer enjoyment and appetite reaches its maximum of bursting exuberance."[64] Lewis, going further, feels that by "piling audacity on audacity," Dunbar is here "playing a practical joke on his audience." [65] And Scott writes that though Dunbar is "outwardly joking," inwardly he is "in earnest" in his feelings of "sexual disillusionment and unhappiness." At the same time, "what is clear," says Scott, is that Dunbar had an audience "which would relish this poem—an audience of women."[66]

To understand the meaning of the poem, we must understand the frame constructed for the three accounts of marriage, since this provides the basis for the developing incongruity and contrast. Coming to "ane gudlie grein garth [garden], full of gay flouris" (3), the narrator overhears "thre gay ladeis" (17), who echo in human terms the splendor of the garden: they are "All grathit [adorned] in to garlandis of fresche gudlie flouris" (18). They are like bright flowers and seem to be part of the natural scene—"Thair mantillis grein war as the gress that grew in May sessoun" (24)—and their faces are as beautiful "as flouris in June" (27):

> Quhyt, seimlie, and soft, as the sweit lillies
> New upspred upon spray, as new spynist [blown] rose;
> Arrayit ryallie about with mony rich vardour,
> That nature full nobillie annamalit with flouris
> Off alkin hewis under hevin, that ony heynd [person] knew.
>
> (28–32)

They even outdo nature—"So glitterit as the gold wer [wire] thair glorius gilt tressis, / Quhill all the gressis did gleme of the glaid hewis" (19–20). The table before them with "ryalle cowpis" full of "ryche wynis" (35) seems in accord with the elegance of the scene. But along with the splendor, the picture painted in the first forty lines is full of ambiguities. For instance, the emphasis on green in the description of the ladies' garb is strange, since this color was not only thought to bring bad luck and to symbolize inconstancy and falseness, it was also a color prescribed for the dress of the lower classes. Moreover, the ladies' hair, combed out and hanging down their backs (21–22), is in a style associated with unmarried girls, not wives or widows.[67]

The ambiguities increase when the women begin to speak, although the narrator has assured us that what he overheard was "hie speiche" and "hautand wourdis," lofty discourse and noble language

(12). Our impression is that the words will echo the "sugarat sound" of the bird's glad song (7) and will complement the "savour sanative," the healthful fragrance, that arises from the "sueit flouris" (8), and the "fresche odour fynest of smell" (33) that envelops the ladies. The beginning of the Widow's initial speech jars with this setting: "Bewrie, said the Wedo, ye woddit wemen ying, / Quhat mirth ye fand in maryage" (41–42). The imperative here is hardly the courtly language we expect, and the reply, coming from "ane lusty," does not seem appropriate to a lady who has been described in terms of such sweet and delicate images. The jarring continues as we are made aware of the contrast between the natural beauty of the garden and the "lewd indecency" of the women, between the richness and elegance of their attire and the grossness of their words, between the commonplaces of allegorical garden settings and the "cynical lechery" described. Though all this is "obvious and calculated," the result, as Wood says, is "wholly original."[68] Taking a different tack, Speirs insists that there is "no essential contrast" between the natural scene and the women, nothing pointing to the beauty of nature and the ugliness of vice: "The hawthorn, the birds and the gossips are filled with the same heady wine, the same exuberance of life; they are equally on the plane simply of nature and instinct."[69] While such a comparison may in itself be valid, Speirs shows little understanding of the late medieval view of man and of sin when he does not realize that man reduced to "instinct" was *de facto* sinful. A better analysis of the contrast is given by Kinsley: "Ideal beauty is revealed as the whited sepulchre of lust, and what seems to be of the bower is seen to belong to the street."[70] At the same time, it should be recognized that the incongruity manifested by this contrast is in accord with the ambiguity marking the poem from its opening lines.

While the three speeches of the women provide three perspectives on love, they are not to be thought of as comprising a love *débat*.[71] As parodies of confessions, these monologues seem to have grown out of the words of Chaucer's Wife of Bath and, earlier, of La Vieille in Jean de Meun's *Roman de la Rose*. It is as though Dunbar broke up a single speech into three parts, as he did in the *Twa Cummeris* when he created two parts. Although the three speeches reveal far more similarities than differences, the first two speakers, the "woddit wemen ying," may be seen as preliminary to the Widow, providing a context for her words, which comprise almost half the number of lines in the poem. The widow acts, moreover, as mistress of ceremonies here, a female equivalent to Chaucer's Harry Bailly, who states the topic of discussion, which apparently has four parts to it: what "mirth" have the wives found in marriage; have they taken lovers; given the opportunity, would they "cheis better"; and, finally—what would seem to be the major issue—is marriage "ane blist band," a blessed bond, that should last until death? (41–48).

The subsequent monologues on the experience of marriage, of the genre entitled the *chanson de la mal mariée*,[72] are remarkably similar not only in details but in the answers they give to these questions. Rather than vary the accounts in any significant way, the poet, it would seem, has chosen to be incrementally repetitious in showing the impotence of the husbands and the scorn, longings, and deceptions of their wives. While these details may function to give a sense of "sheer preposterousness,"[73] and may be enjoyed for their unexpectedness and for the virtuosity they reflect, they also make us feel that although marriage is the subject of the *Tretis*, the main theme points to the gap between appearance and reality that is too frequently the way of the world.[74] Not only do appearances in the frame jar with the reality of the words, the frame also shows the deceptions, especially those hidden under ornate speech, that are revealed in the three confessions that follow.

The first speaker, after cursing marriage as being "agane the law of luf, of kynd, and of nature" (58), imagines what it would be like to be free of her husband, going wherever she wishes and choosing lovers whenever she pleases. But this reverie gives way to the reality of her marriage to an old man:

> I have ane wallidrag, ane worme, ane auld wobat carle,
> A waistit wolroun, na worth bot wourdis to clatter;
> Ane bumbart, ane dron bee, ane bag full of flewme,
> Ane skabbit skarth, ane scorpioun, ane scutarde behind.
>
> (89–92)[75]

Such a passage as this makes meaningful Lewis's description of the *Tretis* as "almost a flyting."[76] When her husband embraces her, this wife feels that she is in the arms of the devil: "Than think I hiddowus Mahowne hes me in armes; / Thair ma na sanyne [blessing] me save fra that auld Sathane" (101–2). Rather than give freely her marriage debt, she charges her husband for the pleasure of lovemaking—"His purse pays richely in recompense efter" (136)—with kerchiefs, gowns, rings, and jewels: "thus I sell him solace, thoght I it sour think" (144).

This first speaker exists in a dreamworld where what is real is not at all clear. She speaks in the conditional—the auxiliaries "micht" and, mainly, "suld" permeate her musing; her thoughts take the form of metaphors and similes—though, ironically, she blames her husband for "Ever ymagynyng in mynd materis of evill" (122)—and her response is rarely what the situation calls for: "Quhen kissis me that carybald [monster], than kyndillis all my sorow" (94). Although she views her husband as "waistit and worne fra Venus werkis, / And may nought beit worth a bene in bed of my mystirs [needs]" (127–28), he is constantly presented as loving his wife. And when he wishes to make love to her, then, says she, "am I dangerus and daine [offish and haughty] and dour of my will" (132). Such incongruities continue in the other ladies' response to this confession— "all thai leuch apon loft with latis [manners] full mery" (147)—although the speaker has hardly been amused by her condition.

The second confession emphasizes even more than the first the gap between appearance and reality. Beginning with the statement of her unhappy marriage, the second wife describes her husband as "a young man ryght yaip [active], bot nought in youth flouris" (170). Like the previously described old husband, he has been "waistit apone wemen" (178), but unlike the other he is uninterested in any kind of lovemaking. Still, he maintains the appearance of being a rake, dressing and flirting like one "mare valyeand in Venus chalmer":

> He semys to be sumthing worth, that syphyr in bour,
> He lukis as he wald luffit be, thocht he be litill of valour;
> He dois as dotit [foolish] dog that damys [waters] on all bussis,
> And liftis his leg apone loft, thoght he nought list pische;
> He has a luke without lust and lif without curage;
> He has a forme without force and fessoun [fashion] but vertu,
> And fair wordis but effect, all fruster [useless] of dedis;
> He is for ladyis in luf a right lusty schadow.
>
> (184–91)

At least an old husband "is at Venus werkis na war na [worse than] he semys" (200). From this criticism the wife goes on to imagine in the manner of the first wife how pleasant it would be to be free of marriage: "Apone sic materis I mus, at mydnyght, full oft, / And murnys so in my mynd I murdris my selfin" (211–12). Finally, she expresses the pretense that is her way of dealing with her husband:

> I cast on him a crabit E, quhen cleir day is cummyn,
> And lettis [pretend] it is a luf blenk [look], quhen he about
>   glemys [glances],
> I turne it in a tender luke, that I in tene warit [anger spent],
> And him behaldis hamely [familiarly] with hertly smyling.
>
> (227–30)

The anguish and hate have increased from the first confession, but again the speech calls up laughter:

> Onone, quhen this amyable had endit hir speche,
> Loudly lauchand the laif allowit [other praised] hir mekle:
> Thir gay Wiffis maid game amang the grene leiffis;
> Thai drank and did away dule [sorrow] under derne bewis.
>
> (239–42)

The Widow's speech, containing the ingredients of the previous monologues, is more a sermon than a confession—or even a parody of a confession, like those of the wives already seen which lack any contrition. The Widow now takes the role of the preacher trying to pierce the "perverst hertis" of sinners:

> God my spreit now inspir and my speche quykkin,
> And send me sentence to say, substantious and noble;
> Sa that my preching may pers your perverst hertis,
> And mak yow mekar to men in maneris and conditiounis.
>
> (247–50)

The irony here is great, for the Widow's parody of pulpit oratory is a perversion of proper advice. Dunbar seems to have chosen a widow as speaker not only because she would necessarily be experienced, having been twice married, but because of the conventional view in his lifetime that after the death of their husbands widows should lead contemplative lives apart from the world, if not actually as religious recluses. The ideal was demonstrated by the "povre widwe" at the beginning of Chaucer's *Nun's Priest's Tale*, and negated by the activities of the Wife of Bath, who, after having five

husbands, was still very much a part of this world. The statement of
intention at the beginning of the Widow's speech in Dunbar's *Tretis*
calls up something of this ideal but actually falls far short of it. The
progression from wives to widow may also be seen as comparable to
the structure of the late Middle English *Parliament of Three Ages*.
There, after Youth and Middle Age argue about which time of life is
the better, Old Age tells them that each is inadequate; for, since
death takes all, they should be putting aside earthly pleasures and
looking to eternal life. Perhaps something of this ideal is parodied in
the *Tretis* in the "sentence . . . substantious and noble" that the
Widow refers to but that is not to be found in her actual words.

After stating the ironic point of her words, the Widow immediately shows her speech for the dissembling it is:

> I schaw you, sisteris in schrift, I wes a schrew evir,
> Bot I wes schene [fair] in my schrowd, and schew me innocent;
> And thought I dour wes, and dane [haughty], dispitous, and bald,
> I' wes dissymblit suttelly in a sanctis liknes:
> I semyt sober, and sueit, and sempill without fraud,
> Bot I couth sexty dissaif that suttillar wer haldin.

(251–56)

How to achieve this dissembling is the "lesson" the Widow
teaches—"Be of your luke like innocentis, thoght ye haif evill myn-
dis" (267)—as she explains how she has had two husbands that held
her dear while she scorned them. Although these men are in many
ways like the two husbands already described, Dunbar seems to use
them to echo features found in the others; and in the way the Widow
treats them we see her going beyond the wives. The perverseness—hating her husbands the more they love her—as well as the
hypocrisy and deception, continues beyond marriage to the state of
widowhood, when the Widow in effect acts out the fantasies and
wishes of the wives; and in her speech we see not only the greatest
gap in the poem between appearance and reality but a gap that is
literally presented as an ideal.

Dunbar goes beyond creating a self-deceiving character, like
Chaucer's Wife of Bath, and presents what may be viewed as a
female version of Chaucer's Pardoner—someone who knows and
flaunts his hypocrisy. And here, even worse, the hypocrisy is in the
form of false teaching—the Pardoner at least, in spite of himself,

caused people to repent. The wives, laughing and praising the Widow, say "thai suld exampill tak of her soverane teching, / And wirk efter hir wordis, that woman wes so prudent." (507–8). Following this affirmation, they pass the night drinking, chatting, and dancing, until with the coming of dawn, everyone, including the narrator, goes home to rest. At the end the setting of the occasion is once again called up in all of its aureate splendor:

> Silver schouris doune schuke as the schene cristall,
> And berdis schoutit in schaw [grove] with thair schill notis;
> The goldin glitterand gleme so gladit ther hertis,
> Thai maid a glorius gle amang the grene bewis.
>
> (515–18)

This return to the frame at the beginning of the poem recalls the Midsummer's Eve setting, which was not in the late Middle Ages the innocuous event a reader of even Shakespeare's *Midsummer Night's Dream* might think. Traditionally, this Eve of St. John, comparable to Halloween, was a time when the supernatural was visible in nature, when "all kinds of supernatural beings, witches, fairies, ghosts, and demons were abroad in particular power and force."[77]

The Midsummer's Eve dating provides an initial and basic detail for understanding the three women and the nature of Dunbar's poem. The time, "neir as midnicht wes past" (2), and the garden, "Hegeit, of an huge hicht, with hawthorne treis" (4) continue the associations with the magical and the supernatural. The women here, drinking their wine at midnight under a holly tree on Midsummer's Eve, seem more like witches than like ordinary mortals—in this sense resembling the loathly lady in Chaucer's *Wife of Bath's Tale*, who is really a shapeshifter. As A. D. Hope has pointed out, the green garb of these "thre gay ladeis" was the traditional attire of elves and fairies, and the light shining from them (19–22) may be a reflection of the fairy light that was thought to illuminate the underworld.[78] The single holly they sit under and the hawthorn hedge surrounding them are likewise associated with the supernatural, the hawthorn supposedly, on the one hand, providing protection from fairies and witches and, on the other, exposing one sitting under it to enchantment.[79]

The narrator here, seeking "mirthis" (9) on this Eve, is hardly celebrating it properly; and his interpretation of what he witnesses, as a "pastance most mery" (526), is hardly adequate.[80] The three women may, notwithstanding the narrator's view, be seen representing a perversion of goodness and chastity, and their Midsummer's Eve festivities the reverse of the proper celebration of a major religious festival.[81] Their view of marriage is, moreover, a demonic equivalent of the Christian sacrament. The poet's emphasis at the end of the poem is on marriage and the nature of women as he asks his question, "Quhilk wald ye waill [choose] to your wif, gif ye suld wed one?" (530), a parody of the conventional medieval *demande d'amour*. This question of love is hardly to be answered. The parody of marriage revealed in this poem has been sufficient for us to see how far the given is from the ideal. And the ideal called up is the right-loving insisted on by Dunbar the cleric and Dunbar the poet.

No matter how entertaining the *Tretis* may be, no matter that it may originally have been designed for performance or court entertainment—at the end the poet addresses "Ye auditoris most honorable, that eris has gevin / Oneto this uncouth aventur" (527–28)— the work goes beyond the *demande d'amour*, beyond, even, the satirical portrayal of wives and of marriage. For all the hyperbole and alliterative excesses, and for all the vulgarities, what is revealed in the monologues is but the way of the world, doubtless recognizable to Dunbar's audience. As the women turned their husbands and marriages into grotesqueries, so, in "celebrating" them, Dunbar continues the grotesquerie. But he has also suggested the ideal beyond the way of the world, most immediately in the Midsummer's Eve setting, for St. John the Baptist, the saint being honored in the Christian feast, is, as Caxton put it in his translation of the *Legenda Aurea*, "master of the school of virtues and of life, the form of holiness, the rule of justice, the mirror of virginity, the ensample of chastity, the way of penance, pardon of sin, and discipline of faith."[82]

For Dunbar to write a poem ostensibly praising the opposites of these virtues is for him to continue writing in the ironic vein seen in "Now of wemen" (no. 45) and, indeed, in all of his celebrations of earthly love. But here, where the praise of that not deserving praise is so blatant, we have the most vivid picture in all of Dunbar's poems of wrong loving, as well as, perhaps, his most effective argument for its opposite, the right-loving stated clearly in "Now culit is Dame Venus brand" (no. 52) and in the debate between the merle and the nightingale (no. 63).

CHAPTER 6

The Craft of the Makar

I *The Spoken Voice*

DOMINANT in Dunbar's poetry is the human voice. While no doubt necessarily present because of the oral nature of this verse, constructed at a time when listening to poetry was still more customary than reading it, the voice provides both a significant poetic device for Dunbar and a noteworthy characteristic of his art. Sometimes, as in the *Flyting of Dunbar and Kennedie* (no. 6) and the *Tretis of the Tua Mariit Wemen and the Wedo* (no. 47), the poem is structured by various voices. But what Dunbar values is the oral element itself, not the possible variations of voice. As has been suggested earlier, the speeches in the *Flyting* are so stylistically similar that they could be viewed as coming from the same speaker; and those of the three women in the *Tretis* seem to be three parts of a single speech. Similarly, in the *Twa Cummeris* (no. 46) what distinguishes one speaker from the other is the subject of the complaint rather than the language or manner of the speech. And in "In secreit place" (no. 28) it is not always easy to tell whether the speaker is the "beyrne" or the "bricht."

This employment of voice may be related to that in the *Canterbury Tales* when Chaucer insists that he is going to tell the tales as the different pilgrims told them. Although he wants us to realize that the Miller's words will be affected by his drunken condition, we are finally aware of a narrating voice that seems closer to Chaucer than to the drunken Miller. Whereas the voices of the speakers in the *Flyting* are different from those in the *Tretis*, the differences are due mainly to the language proper to each poem and not to any desire by the poet to create varied characters or, for that matter, characters at all. Only once does Dunbar create a poem wholly in a voice purporting to be someone else's—"I, Maister Andro Kennedy" (no. 40)—but even here the monologue is not designed so

126

that we may know and understand the speaker, as the "confessions" of Chaucer's Pardoner, Reeve, and Host, for instance, relate to their speakers. Dunbar's monologues—quite different from those of, say, Robert Browning—may be said to make us aware of speaking, not of speaker.

It is, in fact, unusual for Dunbar to write a poem that does not employ a speaking voice, of narrator or of character. In some works we are aware of more than one voice, as in the sequential speeches of the *Flyting* and the *Tretis*, and, in an interesting variation, in "Now lufferis cummis" (no. 22), where after the poet, speaking as an old horse, concludes his petition, we have the sequel, the "*Respontio Regis,*" in which the king grants what has been requested. More than one voice appears also in dialogue form, as in "In secreit place" (no. 28) and the *Merle and the Nychtingaill* (no. 63). But most of Dunbar's poems make use of a single, or a main, voice, generally that of the poet. More accurately, the authorial voice should be viewed as that of the poet's persona, the narrator. Purposefully injected into the poems, even providing a context of sorts for what follows, this voice takes several forms and achieves various effects.

Sometimes the voice of the narrator addresses us directly in the language of the preacher—"Be mirry, man! and tak nocht far in mynd / The wavering of this wrechit warld of sorrow" (no. 73) or "Think, man, thow art bot erd and as!" (no. 74). At other times, through the use of such pronouns as "we," "our," and "us," the narrator joins the audience to him, suggesting, for instance, that the words of admonition are to be applied to both speaker and audience, as in the short piece defining life as "A slyding quheill *us* lent to seik remeid" (no. 76). Such plural pronouns may also imply that the sentiments being presented are those of everyone—as in the expression of grief in the elegy on the death of Bernard Stewart (no. 62), or in that of thankfulness in "Done is a battell on the dragon blak" (no. 81), or in that of praise in "Hale, sterne superne" (no. 82).[1]

In other poems without first-person pronouns we are still aware of listening to the voice of a speaker because terms of direct address are employed in the opening lines, such as "Schir, at this feist of benefice" (no. 11) and "My prince in God, gif the guid grace" (no. 26). In fact, of the eighty-five or so poems making up the Dunbar canon, only the verse essays commonly called *Of Discretioun in Asking* and *Of Discretioun in Geving* (nos. 14–15), along with the attack on Donald Owre (no. 36), seem to have been constructed without taking voice or speaker into account. But these *Discretioun* poems should properly be viewed as forming the first two parts of a three-part essay on *Discretioun*, and it is significant that the third poem in the series, *Of Discretioun in Taking*, begins "Eftir geving I speik of taking" (no. 16). Voice is thus an essential ingredient in this verse essay too.

One effect of Dunbar's insistence that we be aware of a speaker is a sense of the immediate and the personal, frequently juxtaposed against an earlier-established formality. When the poet proceeds as though he is writing an essay—as in the *Discretioun* poems and in the formal definition, "Four maner of folkis ar evill to pleis" (no. 23)—the personal observation and direct address function to change the tone of the work, as well as to anchor the words in reality and keep them from seeming to be conventional moralizing or abstract advice.[2] It may be significant that such a change of pace does not occur in the poem on Donald Owre, for there, where the poet is being totally serious in his condemnation of a man he regards as a dangerous traitor, he directs the attention of his audience from beginning to end wholly on this subject.

The speaking voices of the narrator in Dunbar's poetry may be classified as being by and large of two kinds. The first voice gives the impression of being spoken aloud and is emphasized most noticeably in the various petitions to the king—"Schir, I complane off injuris" (no. 5), for instance—but also in all the poems using direct address. In some instances the address is a formal one and directed at a particular audience—"My Lordis of Chalker, pleis yow to heir / My coumpt" (no. 25) and "O gracious Princes, guid and fair, / Do weill to James your Wardraipair" (no. 34). But Dunbar rarely addresses a single or particular person other than king and queen—generally termed "schir" and "madam"—and an opening like that of the *Flyting* is unusual: "Schir Johine the Ros, ane thing thair is compild" (no. 6). In other instances where the address is to a particular person it is noticeably oblique and metaphorical, as in those poems where the narrator addresses his love: "Sweit rois of vertew and of gentilnes" (no. 49) and "My hartis tresure, and swete assured fo" (no. 50). And in still other instances where the poet speaks in the voice of the preacher, his address is to Everyman: "Be mirry, man!" (no. 73) and "O wreche, be war!" (no. 75). In most instances, however, the address is to a group, as in the complaint to the merchants of Edinburgh, beginning "Quhy will ye, merchantis of renoun" (no. 44) and in the admonition about the proper use of knowledge in the poem addressed to "ye clarkis" (no. 53).

This last poem, "To speik of science, craft, or sapience,"[3] shows particularly well how the voice may enter a verse essay and make abstract and general statements seem concrete, personal, and immediately applicable. The poet begins by citing "everie study, lair, or disciplene" (4) in general and saying that all of these will be wasted if they are not used as they should be. The second stanza focuses in more detail on "The curious probatioun [proving] logicall," "The naturall science philosophicall," "The theologis sermoun, the fablis of poetrie" (9–13), for instance, which are not in themselves worth anything: "Without gud lyfe all in the selfe dois de" (14). From this analysis the transition is then made to man who must lead the "gud lyfe," and the detached analysis of the first two stanzas changes to direct address:

> Quhairfoir, ye clarkis and grittest of constance,
>   Fullest of science and of knawlegeing,
> To us be myrrouris in your governance,
>   And in our darknes be lampis in schyning.
>
> (17–20)

The first-person plural pronouns here allow the poet to personalize and apply his words of instruction and also to compliment the men of learning: they may be "myrrouris" and "lampis" for *us* who ordinarily are in darkness.

Finally, the direct address as used by Dunbar sometimes permits an informal, even a conversational, tone to enter a formal discourse, as in the reference to "my freind" in the midst of instructions about how to dwell in court—"To dwell in court, my freind, gife that thow list" (no. 41)—and in the address to "bredir deir"—"Thairfoir I pray yow, bredir deir"—in "Quho thinkis that he hes sufficence" (no. 70).[4]

Employing this voice that addresses us directly are not only petitions, sermons, and such special forms as the apostrophe to "Blyth Aberdeane, thow beriall of all tounis" (no. 64), but also reports. And it is unusual for these not to contain the narrator's voice in the opening lines, even if only to set the scene for us. "In secreit place," for instance, begins with the poet's writing "I hard ane beyrne say till ane bricht," and then telling the conversation he has overheard. Only infrequently does Dunbar initiate a dramatic situation without insisting that we explicitly hear his narrator's voice, as in "Ane murlandis man of uplandis mak / At hame thus to his nychtbour spak" (no. 43) and "Rycht airlie on Ask Weddinsday, / Drynkand the wyne satt cumeris tway" (no. 46). But although not mentioned in the opening lines of these two poems, the narrator may be seen as implicitly present, acting as an eavesdropper who allows us to join him. So in the moralizing that "All erdly joy returnis in pane," likewise beginning without the narrator—"Off Lentren in the first mornyng, / Airly as did the day up spring, / Thus sang ane bird with voce upplane" (no. 71)—the bird's song would seem to be directed at the narrator as well as at us; and the statement "Thus sang ane bird" could just as well have been "I heard a bird." It would seem that the poet is beginning these three poems much as he does "In secreit place," though there he happens to state the "I." To begin a report directly is not Dunbar's custom, and he does so in only one poem—"Sir Jhon Sinclair begowthe to dance" (no. 32); ordinarily, he both sets the scene and makes us aware of his narrator's voice and presence.

In these reports, as the first lines make clear, the narrator tells of something that has happened to him—"This nycht, befoir the dawing cleir, / Me thocht Sanct Francis did to me appeir" (no. 4)—something that he has done—"Amang thir freiris, within ane cloister, / I enterit in ane oritorie" (no. 80)—something he has heard—"This hindir nycht in Dumfermeling, / To me wes tawld ane windir thing" (no. 27)—or something he is feeling—"I that in heill wes and gladnes, / Am trublit now with gret seiknes" (no. 7). Also, in most of the reports the narrator seems to be confiding in us or telling us something very personal: "This nycht in my sleip I wes agast" (no. 42). His customary tone is more that of a man speaking quietly to a friend than that of a court entertainer performing before a group. Aside from "I, Maister Andro Kennedy," which should be understood as a performance, Dunbar's only poem using the voice of the court entertainer is the burlesque concerning Sir Thomas Norny. Its opening lines show this public quality as the poet acts as minstrel asking his audience for their attention—"Now lythis [listen] off ane gentill knycht" (no. 35)—and in this poem the narrative "I," rather than reflect any personal quality, utters the formulas of the minstrel romance. Opposed to this is the account of the wooing of the lamb by the fox (no. 27) where the narrator humorously tries to distinguish his report from those of other writers: "I will no lesingis put in vers, / Lyk as thir jangleris dois rehers" (43–44).

Related to the reports are the various "character sketches" which Dunbar seems to have been fond of writing. Besides the poems about Norny and Donald Owre (no. 36) and the two pieces playing on James Dog's name (nos. 33, 34) is the description of the "blakmoir." At the beginning we are aware of the poet's voice as he tells us how he has decided on his subject: "Lang heff I maed of ladyes quhytt, / Nou of ane blak I will indytt" (no. 37). This report goes on to be in effect the announcement of a tournament, as the poet, taking the role of herald, states what the rules will be.

Another unusual use of the spoken voice is to be found in the so-called *Dregy of Dunbar* (no. 30). With its parody of the Mass for the Dead it relies on our being aware of the voice of the preacher, but, at the same time, the entire poem seems to be in the form of a letter and is even called "this epistell" (8): "We that ar heir in hevins glory, / To yow that ar in purgatory, / Commendis us on our hairtly wyis" (1–3). The epistolary manner here does not necessarily exclude the voice of the narrator; rather it would seem that this letter was designed to be read aloud.

II *The Inner Voice*

The second speaking voice of the narrator in Dunbar's poetry is, as it were, *sotto voce*, even the voice of someone thinking aloud, musing, for instance, about the state of the world—"Full oft I mus and hes in thocht / How this fals warld is ay on flocht" (no. 69)—or wondering about how to live—"How sould I rewill me or in quhat wys, / I wald sum wyse man wald devys" (no. 9)—or complaining to himself about the unfair way he is treated—"Complane I wald, wist I quhome till" (no. 19). In some instances this voice changes in the course of the poem and becomes a spoken voice. In "Complane I wald" it takes the form of a direct address to the king: "Thairfoir, O Prince maist honorable! / Be in this meter merciabill, / And to auld servandis haff ane E" (67–69). In other poems, however, as in the related "Quhom to sall I compleine my wo, / And kythe [show] my cairis ane or mo?" (no. 21), the voice changes from musing and becomes a prayer to God: "Lord, how sall I my dayis dispone?" (6).

Two poems in particular—"My heid did yak yester nicht" (no. 3) and "I seik about this warld unstabille" (no. 66), both in the same stanzaic form—show an interesting blend of these two voices in their combining reflection with outward expression. Both poems also take a general condition and relate it in personal terms. In the former the condition of "dulnes and distres" (10) centers on the narrator's headache of "yester nicht"; in the latter the narrator is able to understand the "unstabille" and "dessaveabille" nature of this world by realizing that whereas "yesterday" the weather was "soft and fair" and "als fresche as pako fedder," today it stings like an adder (5–9). The state of "yisterday" (11) is developed as the narrator shows his awareness of the "dessaveabille" nature of the world, that what begins one way concludes all to the contrary. The first two stanzas here are marked by the musings of the narrative "I", the last two by statements of the way of the world, especially in the last stanza with its lines in the form of proverbial wisdom. These are like the developed apothegms that make up the bulk of the verse essays which have come from Dunbar's pen.

In "He that hes gold and grit riches" (no. 2), for instance, Dunbar's method is to parallel a series of aphorisms, each one comprising a stanza, in order to demonstrate human perversity:

> He that hes gold and grit riches,
> And may be into mirrynes,
> And dois glaidnes fra him expell,
> And levis in to wrechitnes,
> He wirkis sorrow to him sell.
>
> (1–5)

But then at the end, the poet changes the tone, and the "mirrynes" and "glaidnes" become the totality of his concern:

> Now all this tyme lat us be mirry,
> And sett nocht by this warld a chirry;
> Now, quhill thair is gude wyne to sell,
> He that dois on dry breid wirry [gnaw],
> I gif him to the Devill of hell.
>
> (21–25)

This last stanza is doubtless what allows the poem to be called "a light alliterative drinking song, reminiscent of goliardic verse."[5] But the mention of the "I" in the last line is what most particularly changes the nature of the utterance from the abstract to the personal.

To view Dunbar's use of voice in still another way, we may see his employment of first-person pronouns as allowing a change from the formal or high style to the casual or low style. The resulting mixed style is one in which the poet by and large plays on the juxtaposition, rather than the blend, of the two styles. Such juxtaposition takes many forms, most obviously that of dialogue and debate. And it is surprising that the author of the *Flyting* did not do any more with real argumentation. The only poem in the Dunbar canon that can be called in any sense a debate is the *Merle and the Nychtingaill* (no. 63), but more striking than the voices of the birds arguing about love is that of the narrator who overhears them and who at the end, after reporting their words, tells how remembering the conclusion that "All luve is lost bot upone God allone" comforts him in his life.

A poem showing a mingling of these two voices—the internal and the spoken—as well as one using many of the styles and motifs found throughout Dunbar's poetry is the so-called *Meditatioun in Wyntir* (no. 10).[6] Beginning with a statement that apparently describes the coming of winter, the poem soon relates the "dirk and drublie dayis" of the macrocosm nature to the heaviness of spirit in the microcosm man, here represented by the narrator:

> In to thir dirk and drublie [wet] dayis,
> Quhone sabill all the hevin arrayis
>   With mystie vapouris, cluddis, and skyis,
>   Nature all curage [spirit] me denyis
> Off sangis, ballattis, and of playis.
>
> (1–5)

The songs, ballads, and plays[7] are properly associated with spring not winter, and the "meditatioun" given here, reflecting the "dule spreit" (8) of the narrator, is wholly in accord with the night, wind, hail, and "havy schouris" (6–7) found in nature.

The internal voice of musing reflects the confused state of the narrator's mind:

> I walk [wake], I turne, sleip may I nocht,
> I vexit am with havie thocht;
>   This warld all ouir I cast about,
>   And ay the mair I am in dout,
> The mair that I remeid have socht.
>
> (11–15)

At this point the musing is objectified as allegorical personifications enter the poem, providing additional voices. Despair advises the narrator to find "sum thing quhairon to leif" (18); Patience tells him not to be concerned with the workings of Fortune (23); Prudence says that he should not value what must necessarily pass away (27); Age, that he remember the account he must make of his life (34); and finally Death, that he recognize what awaits all men: "Thair is nane uther way besyde" (40). Although the narrator feels that he is "assayit on everie syde" (16) by these voices, Dunbar gives no psychomachia here, no dramatized conflict of the hopes and fears or desires and hates of the narrator. If anything, the allegorical personifications of the poem are all in accord with each other, the predictably hostile ones giving positive advice and not at all threatening man. Despair counsels, in effect, the opposite of despair, that man must find something to trust in so as to avoid despairing. Age, who addresses the narrator as "my freind" (31) and "brodir" (33), is not to be feared; nor is Death, who is presented as a necessary fact, not an enemy of man. None of these figures is a deceiver, and their words may be taken as good and as comparable to the advice of the obviously helpful Patience and Prudence.

In one sense the passage of time, referred to by Patience in terms of the hourglass of fortune (25), as well as the passage of life, described by Prudence as "A journay going everie day" (30), is the movement of human life to age and death, symbolized at the beginning of the poem by the "dirk and drublie dayis" the narrator feels oppressing him. These comprise for him the dark night of the soul, and he cannot get out from under this cover: "For feir of this all day I drowp" (41). None of the pleasures of the world—"No gold in kist [chest], nor wyne in cowp, / No ladeis bewtie, nor luiffis blys" (42–43)—can keep him from being in mind of his mortality. With the final stanza, however, a change of pace occurs. The coming of summer, even the thought of it, causes the narrator's spirit to lighten; and the poem concludes with a welcoming cry, "Cum, lustie symmer! with thi flowris, / That I may leif in sum disport" (49–50). These final words bring into the poem still another voice, one that seems clearly out of place; for the proper conclusion should be a real understanding by the narrator of life and death. He should realize the truth of what has been told to him by the allegorical figures, that he should not be afraid of death and that he should see the "dirk and drublie dayis" in the context of eternity.

The ending here, on what has been called "a tentative and hesitant note,"[8] may be seen as comparable to that of "He that hes gold and grit riches" (no. 2), where the poet counsels merriment instead of concern about man's predicament; but in the *Meditatioun,* even more so than in this other poem, the hedonistic advice seems empty indeed. Just as mirth, minstrelsy, and play were found to be of no avail to the "dullit" narrator of "My heid did yak yester nicht" (no. 3), so such superficial pleasures can provide no real solution here. In fact, these lines in this *Meditatioun* negate the realization stated by the narrator in "I seik about this warld unstabille" (no. 66) that sorrow is the way of the world. Even though the narrator in the *Meditatioun* sees that after the "dirk mednycht" comes the "mirthefull morrow," he does not realize that beyond this "Nixt efter joy aye cumis sorrow: / So is this warld and ay hes bein."[9] The end of the *Meditatioun,* with its longing for "lustie symmer," thus takes us on to the "dirk and drublie dayis" that are necessarily ahead and to further "havie thocht" that is just as predictable. It is a very ironic ending, showing that although the narrator has actually found the "remeid" he has sought (15), he apparently does not realize it, or at least cannot accept it, and wrongheadedly confuses the temporary respite of "lustie symmer" with the final solution and understanding.

Throughout the poem the contrast between fear and confidence provides a juxtaposition of tones and suggests a dramatic situation, as the narrator, here acting as Everyman, chooses to close his eyes and ears to anything but "disport." The poem is finally more than a "beautiful meditation whose somberness is . . . lightened by the anticipation of summer."[10] While it may very well be "one of the finest poems Dunbar ever wrote,"[11] it is also one of the most ironic. And the poet's use of several voices may be what is primarily responsible for both its success and its meaning.

Not only do Dunbar's poems give the sense of overhearing the musing of the narrator, they also frequently create the impression that the poet is telling us what he himself has overheard. The frames of the *Twa Cummeris* (no. 46) and *Tydingis fra the Sessioun* (no. 43) give such an impression. So, even more, do the first lines of "In secreit place" (no. 28), the *Tretis* (no. 47) and the *Merle and the Nychtingaill* (no. 63). In each of these poems the narrator overhears two people—or birds—talking, and in the *Tretis* he is clearly cast in the role of an eavesdropper. In "Off Lentren in the first mornyng" (no. 71), where the narrator hears the song of a bird, and in "Musing allone this hinder nicht" (no. 8), where he hears "ane voce," even though the words of wisdom seem designed for his ears and for those of his audience, the speeches are still presented as overheard accidentally or by chance.

In "Musing allone" the disembodied voice "that said on hicht, / May na man now undemit be" (4–5) seems to represent some sort of supernatural wisdom instructing man who is not capable himself of seeing the truth. This confident voice "on hicht" contrasts initially with the narrator's silent "musing" of "mirry day"—doubtless merry days past. Not only providing an answer to the musing, it is a spoken voice not a silent one. But as the poem develops, this voice also reflects the words of the envious, those who scorn the narrator; and later, in references to life at court, it seems to be the voice of the narrator if not of the poet himself. The same voice also speaks in the role of James IV, who is quoted as saying "Do weill, and sett not by demying" (49); and finally, in the last stanza where the speaker prays that he will have a place in heaven, the voice is clearly that of the poet. It is as though the "voce" referred to in the first stanza is a vocalization of the narrator's own musing, as though thought itself has come to life; and the subsequent stanzas mingle interior monologue with a sense of actual speech, as well as the narrator's voice with those of court and king. Far more than in "In to thir dirk and drublie dayis," the narrator is "assayit on everie syde" by voices; but here he is apparently able to sort them out and use them and his memory of good instruction as a basis for his future life.

III *"Me Thocht"*

Frequently in Dunbar's poetry the voice of musing provides an element of uncertainty or imprecision that is generally opposed to statements of certainty and fact. This voice is most often heard when the narrator reports a dream he has had and is marked by the expression "me thocht"—it seemed to me. Such assertions are not only in accord with the dreamlike, they also make ambiguous what is being said and function, in effect, to make the reader look carefully at the actions and words of the vision and not rely on the narrator's response to his dream.

The dreamer's assertion, "This nycht, befoir the dawing cleir, / Me thocht Sanct Francis did to me appeir" (no. 4), is shown later in the poem to represent a false impression: "This freir that did Sanct

Francis thair appeir, / Ane fieind he wes in liknes of ane freir"
(46–47). This later statement is one of fact, without the "me thocht";
but then, as the narrator states how the fiend vanished, he says "me
thocht all the hous end he towk" (49), again suggesting an impression that is of dubious validity. And in the final line the narrator's
description of his response—"And I awoik as wy that wes in weir,"
as a man that was in doubt (50)—is not designed to remove ambiguity from the poem.

Confusion marks the entire piece from beginning to end, impres-
sions cannot be trusted, and it is not even clear whether the narrator
responds properly when he rejects the command to "reffus the
warld" and become a friar (5). His rejection is not because of his
awareness of the corruption of friars but, first, because he has heard
that more saints are made of bishops than of friars and would therefore prefer to have "ane bischopis weid" (29); and, second, because
he has already "maid guid cheir" (35) in the garb of a friar: in "the
freiris style" he has used "mony wrink and wyle," many tricks and
wiles, "ay reddy all men to begyle" (41–45). When at this point the
fiend vanishes "with stynk and fyrie smowk" (48), it is not necessarily because the temptation has failed. What has happened or what is
meant is not clear. The narrator's rejection is ambiguous at best, and
along with all the humor is the suggestion that there is no need for
him to be tempted further since he is already damned. Both narrator and audience are to be seen being "in weir" at the end of this
experience and not only because of the possibility that the head of
the Franciscan order is the Devil.

In other dream poems the expression "me thocht" reflects an
element of incredulity or disbelief. In "As yung Awrora, with cristall
haile" (no. 38) the narrator's dream "Off sonis of Sathanis seid" (4) is
presented in the tone of one stating something too amazing to be
true:

> Me thocht a Turk of Tartary
> Come throw the boundis of Barbary,
> And lay forloppin [fugitive] in Lumbardy
> Full lang in waithman [outlaw's] weid.
>
> (5–8)

And likewise in "Lucina schynnyng in silence of the nicht" (no. 39),
the narrator's "havy thocht" (4) and "weirines" (9) produce "ane

dremyng and a fantesy" (10) in which, says the narrator, "Me thocht Deme Fortoun with ane fremmit cheir [strange countenance] / Stude me beforne" (11–12), predicting that his woes will be over when an abbot clothed in eagle's feathers flies up in the air (23–24). Even the narrator recognizes how "nyce [foolish]" (41) this dream is, and he keeps it from everyone until, amazingly, the predicted miracle seems about to happen.

Sometimes Dunbar uses "me thocht" to go beyond the dreamlike and the ambiguous and to suggest through ironic understatement a condition of actuality. Such is the case in "Amang thir freiris, within ane cloister" (no. 80) when the narrator describes the passion of Christ:

> Methocht Judas with mony ane Jow
> Tuik blissit Jesu, our Salvatour,
> And schot [pushed] him furth with mony ane schow [shove],
> With schamefull wourdis of dishonour.
>
> (9–12)

The "me thocht" is used similarly in "This nycht in my sleip I wes agast" (no. 42) when the narrator describes the cursing of mankind: "Dremand me thocht that I did heir / The commowne people bane [curse] and sueir, / Blasfemiand Godis majestie" (21–23). Such swearing is actually commonplace in the world, and the "dremand me thocht" qualification, suggesting perhaps that such swearing could occur only in a fantasy, seems ironic. The reverse of this way of proceeding, though likewise ironic, may be seen in "Doverrit with dreme, devysing in my slummer" (no. 77), when the narrator muses about the corruption that has come to the realm. Here he is describing what is, not what seems to be; the musing, dreamlike as it may seem, is without the "me thocht," and ultimately seems more like direct accusation than like reflection.

In the dream allegories the "me thocht" is found far less frequently than in the other dream poems, though, appearing at the beginning of the allegorical vision in the *Thrissil and the Rois* (no. 55), it serves to emphasize the special otherworld quality of the adventure and provide a springboard for a developed image:

> In bed at morrow, sleiping as I lay,
> Me thocht Aurora, with hir cristall ene [eyes],

> In at the window lukit by the day,
> And halsit [greeted] me, with visage paill and grene;
> On quhois hand a lark sang fro the splene.
>
> (8–12)

But in these dream allegories once the vision is established, there is no hesitation or lack of precision and no use of "me thocht," even at moments when it might well seem appropriate—as in the *Goldyn Targe* (no. 56), when, after Reason is no longer able to defend him from the attack by Love's forces, the dreamer states flatly, "Than was I woundit to the deth wele nere" (208). Here, at least from a literal point of view, a "me thocht" would have seemed both appropriate and desirable. But the phrase does not occur at all in the *Goldyn Targe* or in *Bewty and the Presoneir* (no. 54), the latter representing a special use of the dream in that although the narrator is not seen falling asleep, he is described awakening (45). The ambiguity of the other "realistic" dreams is not to be found in these allegorical visions, where apparently the narrator is transported into a reality beyond the impressionism of "me thocht." Significantly, the phrase is also lacking in the visions of the otherworld represented by "Off Februar the fyiftene nycht" (no. 57) and "Nixt that a turnament wes tryid" (no. 58), as well as in the sequel, the *Amends* (no. 59), where an angel from heaven speaks to the dreamer. Again the emphasis is on a reality beyond this world, and the narrator tells us what he actually saw, not what it seemed to him he saw.[12]

IV *The Movement of Life*

The dreams described by Dunbar join the other reports in providing a story line for his poetry. Although his verse is not properly narrative—as Henryson's, for instance, is—it does employ narrative machinery to create a sense of movement or vitality. Even in a "story" like the fox's seduction of the lamb in "This hindir nycht in Dumfermeling" (no. 27), where the emphasis is on the action itself, not on its being worked out or leading to a climax, the seduction and response are presented as play and game: the fox "with hir playit, and maid gud game" (4). The verbs of action, rather than develop the narrative, function to make the scene in all of its incongruity come to life. In one five-line passage, for instance, the fox is described as having "braisit," "halsit," "schuk," "todlit," "lowrit," and "askit" (8–12). Such verbs are largely responsible for the exuberance and sense of action in "In secreit place" (no. 28), as when it is said of the "beyrne" that "He clappit fast, he kist, and chukkit" (11), activity leading to the "play" that men call "the dery dan" (59–60). They are also what dominate the birds' attack on the flying friar in "As yung Awrora, with cristall haile" (no. 38), making the catalogue of birds—and the concomitant profusion of nouns—come alive: "And evir the cuschettis [wood pigeons] at hym tuggit, / The rukis him rent, the ravynis him druggit, / The hudit crawis his hair furth ruggit [pulled]" (69–71). In this incremental repetition the chaotic sound and the violence come together: "Thay nybbillit [pecked] him with noyis and cry, / The rerd [noise] of thame rais to the sky" (93–94).

This sense of action is produced by means other than the choice of verbs; at times the poet uses verbs as present participles so as to give the sense that something is happening at the moment. When Dunbar writes, for instance, that "Now culit is Dame Venus brand; / Trew luvis fyre is ay kindilland" (no. 52), he not only makes a contrast between the two kinds of love through the juxtaposition of past and present participles, he also gives a sense of immediacy and vitality to "trew luvis fyre." Similarly, when in "To speik of science, craft, or sapience" (no. 53), he says that everything that is not used as it should be is wasted, he expresses the using as something active, being done by man at the moment: "All is bot tynt [lost] or reddie for to tyne [lose], / Nocht using it as it sould usit be, / The craift exerceing [practising], considdering not the fyne [end]" (5–7).

Motion is more than a motif or a point of grammar in Dunbar's poetry; it is, in fact, a dominant characteristic of his art, related to what Edwin Morgan has termed his "restless and nervous force."[13] Sometimes the sense of movement comes from the subject of his poems, as in the several pieces on the mutability of this world and of man's life: "Haif mynd that eild ay followis yowth; / Deth followis lyfe with gaipand mowth, / Devoring fruct and flowring grane" (no. 71, ll. 9–11). Man should realize that such movement, of nature and of fortune's wheel, is a principle of life in this world: "For as thow come sa sall thow pas; / Lyke as ane schaddow in ane glas. / Hyne [hence] glydis all thy tyme that heir is" (no. 74, ll. 4–6). But the movement from life to death—"Quhat is this lyfe bot ane straucht way to deid" (no. 76)—does not have to be man's only movement. In fact, movement is the proper and correct state of man who is an exile from his heavenly home; and he should choose to be the pilgrim returning to this home: "Walk furth, pilgrame, quhill thow hes dayis lycht, / Dres fra desert, draw to thy duelling place" (no. 75, ll. 9–10). Man must disassociate himself from the movement of the world, which is that of death not of life: "Heir nocht abydis, heir standis nothing stabill, / This fals warld ay flittis to and fro" (17–18). His movement, far from necessarily being a reflection or imitation in microcosm of the mutability of the macrocosm, may in its purposefulness be juxtaposed against it: "I seik about this warld unstabille/ To find ane sentence convenabille" (no. 66). The opposite of this activity is despair and the feeling of being overcome by approaching death: "My deathe chasis my lyfe so besalie / That wery is my goist to fle so fast" (no. 50, ll. 15–16).

In other poems movement is Dunbar's way of bringing to life a static cataloging, as in "This nycht in my sleip I wes agast" (no. 42), where the devil passes through the marketplace noting the curses of mankind. And in still others movement provides a touch of humor in what might otherwise seem to be a grave situation. So in "This nycht, befoir the dawing cleir" (no. 4), when the spirit purporting to be St. Francis tries to lay a friar's habit on the dreamer's bed, the dreamer responds with a movement completely unexpected: "Me thocht on bed he layid it me abone, / Bot on the flure delyverly [quickly] and sone / I lap thairfra, and nevir wald cum nar it" (8–10). The movement of the habit is played against the movement of the frightened narrator, and the passage serves to show vividly—more so than would a description of his feelings—the narrator's attitude and the tone of this poem.

Along with hearing the voice of the narrator, we are frequently aware of his movements. We witness him following his lady into her garden—"In to your garthe this day I did persew" (no. 49, l. 6); and at the beginning of the *Tretis* (no. 47), we see how on Midsummer's Eve he "muvit furth allane" (2) beside the hedge of a garden: "I drew in derne to the dyk to dirkin efter mirthis" (9), that is, he moved in secret to the hedge in search of mirth. Elsewhere, however, the narrator's lack of movement is especially noticeable, as in the *Thrissil and the Rois* (no. 55), when "fresche May," standing by the bed of the unwilling dreamer, orders him to "Uprys, and do thy observance" (37), as in the *Dream* (no. 60), where the dreamer, weighed down by Distress and Heaviness (20), cannot leave his bed and join the dance, and as in the *Goldyn Targe* (no. 56), where nature is described as having the vitality of something animate while the narrator seems almost inanimate.

The effect in this poem is the result of Dunbar's presenting nature in terms of a movement more properly human. Even the sunrise is full of motion—"Up sprang the goldyn candill matutyne" (4); the song of the birds seems like a dance, reflecting, as it were, the dance of life—"wyth skippis and wyth hoppis, / The birdis sang upon the tender croppis" (19–20); and even the growth of the flowers is seen here as a matter of noticeable movement—"The rosis yong, new spreding of thair knopis [buds]" (22). Contrasted with all this movement is the state of the narrator: "I raise and by a rosere [rose garden] did me rest" (3). After an initial awakening, he rests and falls asleep. Another poem relying on a connection between the narrator and his world is the *Flyting* (no. 6). At the beginning Dunbar states that should he engage in flyting, his words would disturb all of nature:

> The erd sould trymbill, the firmament sould schaik,
> And all the air in vennaum suddane stink,
> And all the divillis of hell for redour [fear] quaik,
> To heir quhat I sould wryt with pen and ynk.
>
> (9–12)

Dunbar's favorite device for suggesting motion seems to be the dance, and indeed such may be an expression of the sexual activity represented by the "dery dan" of "In secreit place." In some poems dance is merely alluded to—generally in close association with song—but elsewhere dance provides the main structural device, even the main subject. The so-called *Dance in the Quenis Chalmer* (no. 32) is a full expression of dance, and Dunbar not only describes it, he uses its rhythms as, in effect, the poetry of the piece. The rhythms change as the various dancers take to the floor, and may even reflect their stumbling and staggering as well as their hopping and tripping. The dance of the Seven Deadly Sins presented in "Off Februar the fyiftene nycht" (no. 57) may be seen as the same dance as that described in the queen's chamber, but here the dance of the Sins has connotations that are explicitly didactic. Not only representing the pleasures of this world, the dance is also associated with youth, the time when the narrator "wald cast gammaldis [capers] to the sky" (no. 22, l. 8), and in another sense is used to reflect the rhythm of life, as in the *Dream* (no. 60), when "the ladyis danceing in ane trace" (26) try to help the narrator rise from his bed and join them in their dance.

Other means used by Dunbar to provide movement are seen in "Madam, your men said thai wald ryd" (no. 31), where the projected riding forth is contrasted with staying at home. Also the *Dregy* (no. 30) is structured in terms of the projected back-and-forth movement between Edinburgh and Stirling, as well as between purgatory and paradise. The element of movement and contrast is found not only in spatial but also in temporal terms, as in "I that in heill wes and gladnes, / Am trublit now with gret seiknes" (no. 7). And the sense of past in contrast with present time is strikingly seen in "Now lufferis cumis" (no. 22) as the narrator explains his recognition of the differences between his youth and his present state of being an old horse.

V   Sickness and Death

Related to the narrator's voice, as well as to the elements of motion, are those images suggesting the psychological condition of Dunbar's narrator. Most frequently these are images of sickness and lost health, as in "My heid did yak" (no. 3) and in "I that in heill wes" (no. 7), where the narrator's former condition has changed and he is "trublit now with gret seiknes, / And feblit with infermite" (2–3). Also Dunbar uses such a condition as a physical representation of a spiritual or mental condition, as when in "Sanct Salvatour" (no. 1), creating a metaphor for sorrow, he says that if it were not for good hope his "verry corpis for cair wald cleif" (9), that is, sorrow would cause his body to split in two. Silver, he suggests, can best provide a "remeid for this malice" (34), this lack of ease. Similarly, "exces of thocht" does such "mischief" to the narrator of "schir, yit remembir as of befoir" (no. 20) that only the king can "remeid my maledie" (56), and the narrator requests "sum medecyne" (54) from him.

Such metaphorical language continues into other provinces in the poem against "Muris" (no. 5) where the complaint is of "injuris" (1) received, for the poet's meter has been "dismemberit" and "poysonid" (8–9). And in the *Flyting* (no. 6) imagery of sickness and disease is used as a means of invective:

Thow Lazarus, thow laithly lene tramort,
    To all the warld thow may example be,
To luk upoun thy gryslie peteous port,
    For hiddowis, haw, and holkit is thyne ee;
Thy cheik bane bair, and blaiknit is thy ble;
Thy choip, thy choll, garris men for to leif chest;
    Thy gane it garris us think that we mon de.
I conjure the, thow hungert heland gaist.

(161–67)[14]

Moreover, in "As yung Awrora" (no. 38) the improper activities of
Damian are presented especially in terms of his reputed profession
of physician: "He murdreist mony in medecyne" (30).[15]

Healing provides an overall structure to a few poems. In
"Madam, your men said thai wald ryd" (no. 31), becoming healed of
the pox is the ostensible concern of the courtiers. And in several
poems love is presented in terms of sickness and health. In "My
hartis tresure, and swete assured fo" (no. 50) the lady is described as
a "man slayar" (4) who causes the narrator's death; of the wholesome
herbs in the garden of his love in "Sweit rois of vertew" (no. 49), rue
is missing, apparently "slane" (12); and in the *Goldyn Targe* (no. 56)
the narrator is "woundit to the deth wele nere" (208).

Not only would sickness and death seem necessarily to accompany love, they are the actual condition of this world, and it is in this
sense that the narrator's statements of sickness should be taken. As
the bird sings in "Off Lentren in the first mornyng" (no. 71), demonstrating that "All erdly joy returnis in pane," "Heir helth returnis
in seiknes, / And mirth returnis in havines" (25–26). For man who is
"bot erd and as" (no. 74, l. 2) sickness and decay are the normal
condition of his life, and he can look forward to being on this earth
only "Ane ugsum, uglye tramort" (20). To get beyond decay and
corruption, man must look for a healing beyond that provided by
worldly restoratives.

This understanding of world and flesh continues in the various
images of food and eating found in Dunbar's poems. In the *Dregy*
(no. 30), where healing is related to spiritual renewal, Dunbar ironically says that those in penance at Stirling lack "meit restorative"
and "wyn confortative" (11–12)—phrases combining images of
health with those of food and drink, but here clearly confusing
physical and spiritual food. Elsewhere, as in the *Twa Cummeris* (no.
46), the feast of this world is presented as false nourishment; and the

glutton, as may be seen in "Off Februar the fyiftene nycht" (no. 57), is a "fowll monstir," marked by "wame unsasiable and gredy" (91–92) and "surffet and exces" (96). Significantly, in "This nycht in my sleip I wes agast" (no. 42) the purveyors of food and drink— "bakstar," "fleschour," "tavernneir," "maltman," and "browstar" (41–65)—are those who dominate the crafts represented as telling lies in the marketplace.

In other poems—"Schir, at this feist of benefice" (no. 11), for instance—the feast is seen as "no glaid collatioun" (11) when "equale distributioun" (3) is lacking, when those who most need nourishment go unfed. In the companion piece, "Off benefice, Schir, at everie feist" (no. 12) feast and famine are contrasted even more: "Sum swelleis [swallows] swan, sum swelleis duke, / And I stand fastand in a nuke" (6–7). And in "Four maner of folkis ar evill to pleis" (no. 23) the covetous man is presented as the glutton:

> Ane uther dois so dourlie drink,
> And aill and wyne within him sink,
> Quhill in his wame no roume be dry,
> Bot he wald have fra utheris by.
>
> (13–16)

In contrast to earthly food is, as stated in the *Tabill of Confession* (no. 83), the "Haly Supper" of Christ (43). This can give man proper nourishment and medicine, and in releasing him from sin free him from an immersion in the decay and corruption of world and flesh. Such an alteration of man's condition effects a reversal of the ordinary movement from life to death.

VI *The Master Poet*

Any analysis of Dunbar's craftsmanship would be incomplete if it did not show something of the variety of meter and rhyme employed by this "highly conscious technician," this "professional verse-master."[16] Of Dunbar's eighty-four poems only six are written in forms that are not stanzaic. Five of these are in couplets—four in tetrameter lines that are tumbling, run-on, and noun-dense—and are obviously satiric. Of these four, three are complaints against injustice (nos. 17, 19, 29), and one, the *Dregy* (no. 30), is a humorous parody. The fifth poem in couplets, "Now of wemen this I say for me" (no. 45) is slightly different from the others, for it is in pentameter and without blatant overstatement. But the couplet form may be an

initial indication that its apparent praise of women is really to be
viewed as ironic. The other nonstanzaic poem by Dunbar is the
Tretis (no. 47) in long alliterative lines with four stresses per line and
no fixed number of unstressed syllables, a form dating from Old
English times. While found in several Northern romances of the
fifteenth century, the form is nowhere else associated with the
genre of the *chanson de la mal mariée*.

Of Dunbar's stanzaic poems some sixty employ four, five, seven,
or eight lines per stanza; and some fifty use refrains, in the form of
either whole lines or single key words, a practice justifying the
description of Dunbar as "a master of the refrain."[17] No clearly
defined relationship exists, however, between the kind of stanza
used and the total number of stanzas or lines in a poem. That is,
Dunbar apparently did not think of any form in terms of a fixed
number of lines. His five-line stanzas, for instance, are employed in
poems ranging from fifteen to 115 lines in length.

Dunbar's favorite stanzaic form is the tetrameter cinquain rhyming *a a b a b*, with the last line being a refrain. Sixteen poems use
this form[18] while an additional ten are in a related *a a b b a* stanza,
generally with no refrain.[19] These five-line poems defy classification, for Dunbar employs the form, with and without refrain, for
overtly serious and light poems of all kinds. A comparison between
two pieces with the same number of lines and in identical meter will
show something of this variation. "He that hes gold and grit riches"
(no. 2) and "Lang heff I maed of ladyes quhytt" (no. 37) both use the
form *a a b a b* including refrain, and both are twenty-five lines long.
In each the stanzas are generally constructed by means of a single
sentence developed through the use of clauses introduced by
"And", which culminate in the refrain. But notwithstanding these
real similarities in form and method, "He that hes gold" is an ironic
statement of human perversity without any obvious humor, at least
until the somewhat ambiguous last stanza, whereas "Lang heff I
maed" is an out-and-out spoof, a study in burlesque from beginning
to end.

Even more striking is the disparity between "Quho thinkis that he
hes sufficence" (no. 70) and "Madam, your men said thai wald ryd"
(no. 31). Both also employ the *a a b a b* tetrameter stanza with
refrain, and both are thirty-five lines long. But the first piece is a
verse essay on the need for man to be content about his earthly
possessions—"He hes anewch that is content"—whereas the second

is a bawdy and humorous study of fornication and venereal disease—the "libbin of the pockis" of the refrain—with no overtly moral sense.[20] A similar opposition may be found in "I seik about this warld unstabille" (no. 66) and "My Lordis of Chalker, pleis yow to heir" (no. 25). Both are in tetrameters rhyming *a a b b a* without refrain, and both are twenty lines long. But the former is a poignant lament about mutability, and the latter a playful statement of the narrator's penury.

The four-line tetrameter stanza rhyming *a a b b* including refrain is a form in which Dunbar wrote eleven poems ranging in length from twenty-four to one hundred lines,[21] indicating again that no inherent relationship exists between stanzaic form and length of poem. Also these quatrains show the same range of subject and tone as the cinquains. For instance, "Off Lentren in the first mornyng" (no. 71) and "Man, sen thy lyfe is ay in weir" (no. 72), both forty lines long, are serious moralizings; but "Betuix twell houris and ellevin" (no. 59)—the so-called *Amends* to the tournament between tailor and cobbler—also in forty lines, is a humorous satire. Although it may be said that the longer poems in quatrains have obviously serious purposes—for instance, "I that in heill wes and gladnes" (no. 7) and "This waverand warldis wretchidnes" (no. 13) are both one hundred lines long and both concerned with mutability—it does not follow that the shorter poems in quatrains are necessarily light or comic. For instance, whereas Dunbar's prayer to the king that he be Joan Thomson's man (no. 18) and his welcome to the lord treasurer (no. 24) are both joking poems and both in thirty-two lines, his verse-essay "Four maner of folkis ar evill to pleis" (no. 23) is an overtly serious poem and in twenty-eight lines.

Dunbar's seven-line tetrameter stanzas rhyming *a a b b c b c* are, on the other hand, all comic or satiric. The complaint against "muris" (no. 5), the account of the fox's seduction of the lamb (no. 27), "In secreit place" (no. 28), and the report of the dance in the queen's chamber (no. 32)—all having a varying number of lines—are obviously humorous; and only the account of corruption at the Court of Session, "Ane murlandis man of uplandis mak" (no. 43), is essentially satiric and without obvious humor. Dunbar also uses a seven-line stanza with satiric effect in his complaint to the merchants of Edinburgh, but in this poem the form is intricate and unique—*a a a b b a b*, with all the lines in tetrameter but the fifth, which is in dimeter.

Dunbar also uses the seven-line pentameter stanza rhyming *a b a b b c c*—known as the Chaucerian stanza or rhyme royal—in four poems, all having a different total number of lines. This is the dominant verse form for serious and courtly poetry of the fifteenth and early sixteenth centuries, and Dunbar's use of it in the courtly allegorical epithalamion, the *Thrissil and the Rois* (no. 55), is wholly within the established tradition, as is his use of the form in the overtly didactic study of penance, "O synfull man, thir ar the fourty dayis" (no. 84), and in his one-stanza moralizing *Of Lyfe* (no. 76). On the other hand, he uses the built-in stateliness of rhyme royal for comic effects in "My hartis tresure, and swete assured fo" (no. 50), with its exaggerated statement of a lover's grief.

Dunbar's sixteen poems using an eight-line stanza rhyming *a b a b b c b c* with refrain, a form originating with the French ballade, are by and large serious and seem to be wholly in accord with his efforts in rhyme royal. Such is especially true of the thirteen poems in pentameter[22] which range from celebrations, like the Bernard Stewart poems (nos. 61, 62) and the praise of Aberdeen (no. 64), to statements of moral advice, like "To dwell in court, my freind, gife that thow list" (no. 41), to full presentations of Christian doctrine, like "To The, O mercifull Salviour, Jesus" (no. 83). Of the three eight-line stanzaic pieces in tetrameter, two (nos. 74, 80) are likewise serious; but one, the dream allegory *Bewty and the Presoneir* (no. 54), seems less weighty than the others. The main exception to the stateliness of this form, however, is the *Flyting of Dunbar and Kennedie* (no. 6), where Dunbar may be intentionally perverting the usual application of the form even though the poem lacks the refrain typical of the other eight-line stanzas and even though the last quatrain of most of its stanzas is altered to *b c c b*. Dunbar also uses an eight-line tetrameter stanza for comic effects in another piece, "I, Maister Andro Kennedy" (no. 40); but though beginning with alternating rhyme, the rhymes of the second quatrain vary considerably and frequently result in a stanza using only two rhymes, most noticeably in the final stanza where the octave is expanded to twelve lines.

If any verse form represents for Dunbar the vehicle for comedy, it is the tail-rhyme stanza, where a group of rhymed lines in one meter is followed by a shorter line usually in a different rhyme. The most common expression of the form in medieval English literature, a six-line stanza rhyming *a a b c c b*, with two tetrameters followed by a trimeter, is used by Dunbar in his playful picture of Sir Thomas Norny (no. 35). This tail-rhyme stanza is expanded to an eight-line version in the study of inconstancy in love, "Quha will behald of luve the chance" (no. 51), where with an *a a a b a a a b* rhyme scheme three lines of tetrameter are followed by one in dimeter. This poem is additionally special in that it employs the same two rhymes throughout its three stanzas. Further predictable developments of the tail-rhyme stanza occur in the humorous account of the dance of the Seven Deadly Sins and its sequel concerning the tournament in hell (nos. 57, 58), where the form is a twelve-line stanza rhyming *a a b c c b d d b e e b*, with two tetrameters followed by a trimeter, and in the satirical *Feyneit Freir of Tungland* (no. 38), where the basic stanza form uses sixteen lines, rhyming *a a a b c c c b d d d b*, etc., with three tetrameters followed by a trimeter. The first and last stanzas of this poem are expanded to twenty lines in the same form.

For purposes of comic effect Dunbar also uses verses employing internal rhyme, as at the end of each poet's performance in the *Flyting* (no. 6),[23] but most notably in the satire on the lady solicitors: "Thir ladyis fair, That makis repair / And in the court ar kend" (no. 48). Here in eight-line stanzas of alternating tetrameter and trimeter, rhyming *a b a b c d c d*, each tetrameter line uses internal rhyme to give a lightness to the satire. But Dunbar uses what is in effect the same form and principle in his praise of the Virgin, "Hale, sterne superne! Hale, in eterne, / In Godis sicht to schyne" (no. 82). Although in this poem the stanza is developed to twelve lines rhyming *a b a b a b a b c b a b*, including a Latin refrain as the *c* line, the initial octave with its internal rhyme is the same as the stanza used in the satire "Thir ladyis fair." Here, however, the effect is quite different, suggesting in its aureation richness and splendor, not lightness and a sense of irony.

A similar employment of a single form with opposite effects occurs in "Now lufferis cummis with larges lowd" (no. 22) and "Now culit is Dame Venus brand" (no. 52). Both are constructed in six-line tetrameter stanzas rhyming *a a a b b b*, but whereas the first is a humorous study in pathos with Dunbar presenting himself as an old horse, the second is a straightforward statement of true love as opposed to "feynit lufe." Another six-line stanza, but one especially complicated, is found in the attack on Donald Owre (no. 36). Rhyming *a a b b b a* with the initial couplet in tetrameter, the central triplet in trimeter, and the final line in dimeter, the poem creates an effect of consistent shortening, so that each stanza resembles a funnel in its structure. Dunbar's metrical experimentation thus appears in both comic and serious poems, and the one work singled out for praise by Lindsay in his comments on Dunbar in the *Testament of the Papyngo*, the *Goldyn Targe* (no. 56), may be the most demanding of his various poetic forms. Using a nine-line pentameter stanza rhyming *a a b a a b b a b* for a total of thirty-one stanzas, it may very well represent the pinnacle of his artistic achievement.

VI *Conclusion*

What may be concluded from this analysis of Dunbar's poems and poetry are, first, that generalizations about the man and his work are probably more inadequate than helpful; second, that attempts to impose modern categories on his verse have too frequently been misleading and have hindered understanding; third, that Dunbar was a conscious artist whose poems cannot be understood by appealing to what is known—or surmised—about the man himself; and, fourth, that for all its newness Dunbar's verse was grounded in medieval poetic and doctrinal traditions.

That Dunbar's corpus consists mainly of short pieces may explain in part why he cannot easily be encompassed and classified. No subject or theme can be singled out as especially typical of him, and, likewise, no metrical form or rhythm may be held up as his customary vehicle. In what would seem to be favorite forms, the so-called begging poems, for instance, it is finally not at all clear what or how much is to be taken at face value; and in favorite metrical forms like the five-line stanza with refrain, the variations in tone and in effect are greater than the similarities. We may associate Dunbar with certain kinds of writing—flyting, comic dialogue, aureate allegory, long-line alliteration—but we do so essentially because his accomplishment in these forms is so striking, not because they represent him at his most typical.

Dunbar was, to be sure, a master of language, interested in various ways of employing and structuring his Scottish vernacular; and his main achievement may be thought of as the shaping of finely wrought poems. To say this, however, is not to imply that meaning is insignificant or irrelevant in his writings. A moral sense and a wish to celebrate the truths and values of his faith permeate his work and, while going hand in hand with the linguistic and rhythmical effects, are actually the basis of the poetry. Although Lindsay had praised "Dunbar, quhilk language had at large,"[24] emphasizing, it would seem, the copious, varied, and unconstrained expression, the "language" would, at least from the point of view of Dunbar the cleric, have been only empty jangling if it were not for the substance it expressed.

The sense of movement and energy in Dunbar's verse—the result of his "large" or unconstrained play of language—may be seen reflecting the restlessness that the poet-cleric would have viewed as the proper condition of man in this world, as well as giving a sense of joy and possibility in accord with the Christian virtues of faith and hope. Far from being ultimately satirical, despondent, or even homiletic, Dunbar's poetry asks for man's participation in the movement of life. And the poet's essential voice, present regardless of any particular vocal expression, is that of the singer. Noticeable to varying extents throughout his writings, this voice is most pronounced in his praise of the Virgin (no. 82) and in his celebration of Christ's Nativity (no. 79), where the line "Be myrthfull and mak melody" (52) states what all creation, especially all good Christians, should do. This statement may furthermore be seen as a relevant description of what in fact Dunbar himself has done throughout his verse. Ranging from the coarse to the sublime, the mirth and melody serve to lead men to understanding and make the efforts of Dunbar the poet wholly in accord with those of Dunbar the cleric. The result is also a poetry still resonant and compelling.

Notes and References

Chapter One

1. See John Speirs, *The Scots Literary Tradition: An Essay in Criticism*, 2d ed. (Edinburgh, 1934), p. 54; and Arthur K. Moore, *The Secular Lyric in Middle English* (Lexington, Ky., 1951), p. 195.

2. G. Gregory Smith, *The Transition Period* (Edinburgh, 1900), p. 52.

3. Moore, p. 195.

4. Ibid., pp. 195–216.

5. All quotations from Dunbar according to *The Poems of William Dunbar*, ed. W. Mackay Mackenzie (London, 1932; repr. 1960). Poems will be cited by the number given in this edition.

6. See also Dunbar's praise of the three poets in his *Goldyn Targe* (no. 56), lines 253–70.

7. James Kinsley, *Scottish Poetry: A Critical Survey* (London, 1955), p. 32.

8. C. S. Lewis, *English Literature in the Sixteenth Century, Excluding Drama* (Oxford, 1954), p. 97; Speirs, in something of an overstatement, feels that "he is in fact as different from Chaucer as it was possible for another medieval poet to be" (p. 54).

9. Denton Fox, "The Scottish Chaucerians," in *Chaucer & Chaucerians. Critical Studies in Middle English Literature*, ed. D. S. Brewer (University, Ala., 1966), pp. 186–87.

10. Kinsley, p. 32.

11. Lewis, p. 97.

12. Fox, p. 187.

13. See P. H. Nichols, "William Dunbar as a Scottish Lydgatian," *PMLA* 46 (1931), 214–24; and Nichols, "Lydgate's Influence on the Aureate Terms of the Scottish Chaucerians," *PMLA* 47 (1932), 516–22.

14. See, e.g., Ronald D. S. Jack, "Dunbar and Lydgate," *Studies in Scottish Literature* 8 (1970–71), 220.

15. Cf. Christopher Brookhouse, "Deschamps and Dunbar: Two Elegies," *Studies in Scottish Literature* 7 (1970), 123.

16. Janet M. Smith, *The French Background of Middle Scots Literature* (Edinburgh, 1934), p. 77.

17. See, e.g., G. Gregory Smith, "The Scottish Chaucerians," in *Cambridge History of English Literature*, ed. A. W. Ward and A. R. Waller (Cambridge, 1908), II, 258.

18. A. M. Kinghorn, "Dunbar and Villon—A Comparison and a Contrast," *Modern Language Review* 62 (1967), 208.

19. See especially the discussion in Lewis, pp. 66–119.

20. Smith, *Cambridge History*, pp. 239–40.

21. G. Gregory Smith, *Specimens of Middle Scots* (Edinburgh, 1902), p. xiii.

22. Ibid., p. xi; see the main characteristics, pp. xvi–xlix.

23. Smith, *Transition*, p. 51.

24. Ibid., pp. 52–53.

25. On the two poets, see Smith, *Cambridge History*, pp. 257–58; and Lewis, p. 97.

26. Lewis, p. 97.

27. *The Poems of William Dunbar*, ed. John Small, intro. A. J. G. Mackay (Edinburgh, 1893), I, lxxvii; see the comparable classification in Mackenzie, pp. vii–ix.

28. STS, I, cxlii.

29. Lewis, p. 98.

30. Fox, p. 180.

31. Mackay, I, lxxiv.

32. Samuel Marion Tucker, *Verse Satire in England before the Renaissance* (New York, 1908), p. 196.

33. Moore, p. 214.

34. Ibid., p. 196.

35. Smith, *Transition*, p. 53.

36. John Leyerle, "The Two Voices of William Dunbar," *University of Toronto Quarterly* 31 (1962), 316.

37. Edwin Morgan, "Dunbar and the Language of Poetry," *Essays in Criticism* 2 (1952), 156.

38. Lewis, p. 97.

39. Smith, *Transition*, pp. 54–55; cf. Speirs: "Dunbar's mirth is often of a violent character" (p. 67).

40. Leyerle, p. 323.

41. Smith, *Transition*, pp. 57–58.

Chapter Two

1. Mackenzie, *Poems*, pp. xviii–xix.

2. This along with the following evidence is recorded by Mackay in his introduction to the Scottish Text Society edition of Dunbar, I, cliv–clvi.

3. See, e.g., J. W. Baxter, *William Dunbar. A Biographical Study* (Edinburgh, 1952), p. 85.

4. It has been said that the regular prefix of "Maister" to Dunbar's

name in the records implies that he was a master of arts; see Mackenzie, p. xx. On the argument of figuring Dunbar's birth date on the basis of this information, see especially Denton Fox, "The Chronology of William Dunbar," *Philological Quarterly* 39 (1960), 413–25.

5. Commonly referred to as *Quhen the Governour Past in France*—a title based on the colophon in the Maitland folio manuscript and apparently first given the poem by John Pinkerton in his edition of *Ancient Scotch Poems* in 1786—the poem is ascribed to Dunbar only in the Maitland folio manuscript. Although its stanzaic pattern and refrain are characteristic of Dunbar's work, "its inversions, awkwardness, and roughness contrast sharply with his usual direct expression and smoothness, as do the abstract diction, lack of imagery, and deadly serious tone in treating a subject which lends itself to satire. . . . If it was written by Dunbar, it demonstrates a noticeable decline in his poetic ability" (Florence H. Ridley, "Middle Scots Writers," in *A Manual of the Writings in Middle English, 1050–1500*, ed. Albert E. Hartung [New Haven, 1973], IV, 1039). See also the analysis by Denton Fox, who concludes that the poem is not by Dunbar and that he had died close to 1513 ("Chronology," esp. pp. 421–24).

6. Lines 17–18, ed. John Small, Early English Text Society, Original Series 19, 2d ed. (London, 1883), p. 223. Lindsay speaks mainly of Walter Kennedy, Dunbar, and Gavin Douglas. If Lindsay listed the poets in chronological order of their deaths, Dunbar's must have occurred before September, 1522, when Douglas died.

7. *Poems*, ed. Small (1893), I, xv–lxviii; see also J. Schipper, *William Dunbar, sein Leben und seine Gedichte* (Berlin, 1884), pp. 58–103.

8. Mackenzie, p. xix; other scholars, Ridley, for instance, feel that 1455–57 is a more likely date for Dunbar's birth (Ridley, p. 1006).

9. Mackenzie, p. xix; Fox points out that Edinburgh was in the path of the eclipse of 1502, and since the *Flyting* was "probably written between 1500 and 1505," this reference may be "one of the many topical allusions of the poem" ("Chronology," p. 415).

10. Mackenzie, p. xxiii.

11. This poem is commonly referred to as *How Dumbar Wes Desyrd to Be ane Freir*, a title taken from the colophon in the Bannatyne manuscript and first given the poem by Lord Hailes in his edition of *Ancient Scottish Poems* from the Bannatyne manuscript in 1770, David Laing's title, *The Visitation of St. Francis* would, however, seem to reflect the poem's contents more accurately (*The Poetical Works of William Dunbar*) Edinburgh, 1834).

12. See, e.g., *The Poems of William Dunbar*, ed. J. Schipper (Vienna, 1891–94), pp. 237–38; and Baxter, pp. 28 ff. Cf. A. G. Rigg, "William Dunbar: the 'Fenyeit Friar'," *Review of English Studies* 14 (1963), 269–73, who, showing that the theme of the feigned friar is an accepted literary device, casts doubt on such biographical reconstruction.

13. Title from Maitland colophon, first given by Pinkerton. The queen's chamber is not mentioned anywhere in the poem.

14. Tom Scott, *Dunbar. A Critical Exposition of the Poems* (Edinburgh, 1966), p. 162.

15. See the notes to the STS edition (ostensibly all by W. Gregor, but after p. 246 by Mackay), III, 285.

16. On Musgrave see Mackay, I, ccl–ccli; with no evidence at all scholars have even conjectured that she was the subject of two other poems by Dunbar, "Sweit rois of vertew" (no. 49) and "My hartis tresure" (no. 50). See the discussion in Ridley, p. 1021.

17. This is apparently a reference to James Dog, keeper of the queen's wardrobe and the subject of two other poems by Dunbar, nos. 33, 34.

18. Line 60. Of the "dirrye dantoun" Mackay writes, "A dance now unknown" (STS, III, 285).

19. Cf. *William Dunbar. Poems*, ed. James Kinsley, Clarendon Medieval and Tudor Series (Oxford, 1958), p. 130.

20. Scott, p. 162.

21. Ibid.

22. Baxter sees Dunbar speaking "from the heart-strings" (p. 161). France in this poem may have additional comic purposes. Besides the reference in l. 34, the dance is begun by a knight who was "new cum owt of France" (2).

23. E.g., Scott, p. 134.

24. According to Moore, the poem is "of little intrinsic merit"; its historical interest "rests on the assertion of purely personal emotion as fitting matter for poetry" (p. 207).

25. Baxter, p. 133; cf. Scott, p. 134.

26. Baxter, p. 133.

27. Laing's full title contained the addition "To the King." The poem appears only in the Reidpeith manuscript, where there is no colophon.

28. *Canterbury Tales*, A 1373–76, in *The Works of Geoffrey Chaucer*, ed. F. N. Robinson, 2d ed. (Boston, 1957). See also John Livingston Lowes, "The Loveres Maladye of Hereos," *Modern Philology* 11 (1913–14), 527, n.

29. Lines 1–29.

30. See, e.g., Mackay's note in STS, III, 339.

31. See Kinsley, *Poems*, p. 158.

32. Schipper, *Poems*, translates "for" as "to": "the 'curage' [mind] will not awake me in any way to mirth" (p. 234).

33. Ibid., p. 233.

34. *Meditatioun in Wyntir*, title from Pinkerton.

35. E.g., Scott, p. 247.

36. This stems from the postscript in the Chepman and Myllar print of 1508; see Small, *Poems*, STS, II, 51. Hailes in 1770 is apparently the first editor to call the piece *Lament for the Deth of the Makaris*. Whereas

Hailes's title is inadequate in that it "underlines only one phase in this poetic *danse macabre*" (Kinsley, *Poems*, p. 123), so *Quhen He Wes Seik* takes too literally the poet's words in the first stanza. Although it might be argued that the Chepman and Myllar print was published when Dunbar was still alive and should therefore be taken as authoritative, the edition is hardly definitive. Of the seven poems it attributes to Dunbar, for instance, one, the *Ballad of Kynd Kittok*, is no longer accepted as being in his canon. A more accurate title is that given by Allan Ramsay in his 1724 edition—*On the Uncertainty of Life and Fear of Death, or a Lament for the Loss of the Poets*—though, significantly, Ramsay's version omits the first stanza. Also more accurate is the title *The Fear of Death Confounds Me* given by R. T. Davies in his modern collection of *Medieval English Lyrics* (London, 1963), a translation of the Latin refrain.

37. Such a dating, however, contradicts the evidence in other stanzas; see the discussion in Baxter, pp. 133–34.

38. Ibid., p. 134; see also Schipper, *Poems*, pp. 284–85; and Ridley, p. 1009.

39. Scott, p. 250.

40. Ibid., p. 251.

41. Sarum Breviary, II, 278; cf. Ps. 114:3. Cf. Lydgate's "So I Lay the Other Night" and the sixteenth-century lyric beginning "Alas, my hart will brek in three: / Terribilis mors conturbat me" (Davies, p. 170).

42. Speaking of this list of poets, Schipper writes that "though interesting from an historical and literary point of view," it is "much too long for an effective poem" (*Poems*, p. 285).

43. "Remeid", repeated at the end of each stanza, acts here as the equivalent of a refrain.

44. Pinkerton called the poem *Againis Mure, to the King*, a title echoed in Laing's 1834 edition, *Complaint against Mure*. Small conflates these two titles into *Complaint to the King aganis Mure* and is followed by Schipper and Mackenzie.

45. Mackay, STS, I, ccl.

46. Scott, pp. 120–21. Mackenzie, however, would like the apparently mangled *Devillis Inquest* (no. 42) to be the work of Mure (p. 239).

47. Scott, p. 120.

48. Ridley, p. 1008.

49. Cf. the "murlandis man of uplandis mak" (no. 43, l. 1), glossed by Schipper as "a man residing in the moors, with the manners of a highlander" (*Poems*, p. 79).

50. *Canterbury Tales*, A 725 ff.; see also the beginning of the *Miller's Tale*, where Chaucer reaffirms that he should not be held responsible for the "harlotrie" being told (A 3171 ff.).

51. Lines 15159 ff.

52. *Conclusione dell'autore*; see also Chaucer's *Nun's Priest's Tale*,

where the speaker, criticizing "wommenes conseille," says "Thise been the cokkes wordes, and not myne" (B² 4455).

53. Baxter, p. 128.

54. Schipper, *Poems*, p. 226.

55. Moore, p. 199.

56. *Canterbury Tales*, B 47 ff.

57. Ibid., B² 2109 ff.

58. Scott, p. 323.

59. See nos. 27, 28, 32, 43.

60. Scott, p. 121.

61. See, e.g., Mackenzie, p. vii; and Ridley, p. 1011. Mackay refers to them as "precatory poems" or "petitions to the king or queen" (STS, I, cxxi).

62. As Lewis points out speaking of Dunbar's petitions, "Of all the poems which he wrote in this (at first sight) unattractive *genre* hardly one lacks some outstanding excellence" (p. 93).

63. Scholars might have done well to note G. G. Smith's perceptive remarks in 1900 on Dunbar's writing petitions with tongue in cheek (*Transition*, p. 55). Also these petitions show so little of the variety in versification marking Dunbar's poetry in general that it may seem as though Dunbar "had worked out a set pattern in which to address the king, had established a set form for his petitions." See T. S. Dorsch, " 'Of Discretioun in Asking.' Dunbar's Petitionary Poems," in *Chaucer und seine Zeit. Symposion für Walter F. Schirmer*, ed. Arno Esch (Tübingen, 1968), p. 287.

64. *Complaint to the King*, title apparently from Small; Pinkerton and Laing call the piece *Dunbar's Complaint*.

65. Speaking of the inadequacy of Modern English in translating such a passage, John Leyerle nevertheless offers a good rendition: "Only foul, chamber-pot-headed jaillers, / Idle beggers and blackguard raillers, / Grooms, flatterers, and stuttering crones, / Wild gluttons, gut-stuffers and drones, / Drunkards, dicers, bankrupts, imbeciles, / Misguided minions of Mammon's evils" ("Two Voices," p. 322).

66. Baxter, p. 147.

67. See, e.g., Chaucer's so-called *Complaint to His Purse*.

68. Ridley, p. 1014.

69. Dorsch, taking it at face value, calls this "one of the most tactless of Dunbar's poems," and says the tone early in it "could hardly have disposed James to lend a sympathetic ear to its final appeal." He concluded that here and elsewhere if Dunbar "had been able to control his feelings and tongue more firmly," he might have been more successful with his petitions (pp. 290, 292).

70. Smith, *Transition*, p. 55; see the discussion in Ridley, p. 1014. Scott feels that, having tried a variety of approaches to the king, Dunbar is here "trying the approach of outraged virtue expressed in ingenious flyting" (p. 98).

71. Scott, p. 98.

72. *None May Assure in this Warld,* title from Hailes.

73. *Of the Warldis Instabilitie,* title from Pinkerton.

74. Pinkerton makes *To the King* the subtitle of the poem.

75. *To the King, That He War Johne Thomosunis Man,* title from Laing, probably based on Pinkerton.

76. *Welcome to the Lord Treasurer,* title from Laing.

77. This humor is continued in what may be a sequel, "My Lordis of Chalker, pleis yow to heir *(To the Lordis of the Kingis Chalker,* no. 25, title from Laing), when the poet says that the lords of the exchequer need not tire themselves reckoning his rents, rooms, and income, for although he received a sum of money from the lord treasurer, he has somehow spent it and now has only a light purse.

78. *The Petition of the Gray Horse, Auld Dunbar,* title from Laing. Pinkerton called the piece *Lament to the King.*

79. Because of this request the poem has naturally been seen related to the 1506–7 entries in the treasurer's accounts of Dunbar's receiving money for new clothes at Christmas.

80. For a summary of views on this stanza, see Baxter, p. 151.

81. Ridley, p. 1016.

82. Schipper points to its "humorous and amiable tone" *(Poems,* p. 274).

83. Moore, p. 211.

84. *To the King* (title from Hailes), ll. 1–3.

85. This is according to the Maitland manuscript; the Bannatyne version reads, "biddis my brydill ren3e"; see Small, *Poems,* STS, II, 106.

86. Cf. the end of "Schir, ye have mony servitouris," no. 17.

87. "Fredome, honour, and nobilnes" *(Of Covetyce,* title from Hailes, based probably on that in Ramsay), ll. 41–44.

88. *All Erdly Joy Returnis in Pane,* no. 71 (title from Hailes), ll. 13–14.

89. *Best to be Blyth,* title from Hailes.

90. Scott, p. 256.

91. *No Tressour Availis without Glaidnes* (title from Laing, based on Hailes), ll. 1–2.

92. Scott, p. 255.

93. Ibid.

94. See Mackay, STS, I, clvii ff., though the chronology offered here is not to be taken as definitive. More recently Fox has argued persuasively that Dunbar composed in effect all his poems between 1500 and 1513 ("Chronology," pp. 413–25).

95. Scott, pp. 255–56.

96. *Of Discretioun in Asking,* title from Ramsay.

97. "To speik of gift or almous deidis" (no. 15); "Eftir geving I speik of taking" (no. 16).

98. It is difficult to see them aimed at educating the king, as Scott suggests, p. 149.

99. *To the King,* title from Hailes.

100. See Gregor, STS, III, 208; and Baxter, p. 60.

101. See Scott, p. 93.

102. Ibid., p. 94.

103. Title from Laing. I alter Mackenzie's punctuation of the first line; see also Scott, pp. 135–36.

104. Mackay, STS, I, clviii.

105. Ridley, p. 1018.

Chapter Three

1. On James and his court, see, e.g., *The Days of James IIII, 1488–1513,* ed. G. Gregory Smith (London, 1900), especially the account of the Spanish ambassador, Pedro de Ayala, in a letter to Ferdinand and Isabella in 1498 (pp. 54–56). Smith describes James's court as representing in some respects "a kind of carnival before the Lenten sadness of the sixteenth century" (*Transition,* p. 48).

2. *Twelfth Night,* III, i, 62–63.

3. "Renownit, ryall, right reverend, and serene" (*The Ballade of Lord Bernard Stewart, Lord of Aubigny,* title from Chepman and Myllar).

4. In Baxter's view, "It is an entirely laudatory poem and, deprived of its accompaniments of trumpets and blazonries, loses much, there being little in it of intrinsic interest, so formal is the language of ceremonial welcome" (p. 175).

5. "Illuster Lodovick, of France most Cristin king" (*Elegy on the Death of Bernard Stewart, Lord of Aubigny,* title apparently from Laing).

6. Schipper feels that this lament contains language "not ornate and more natural " than that found in the *Ballade,* and that it is consequently "of much greater poetical value" (*Poems,* p. 295).

7. Laing's title, varying Ramsay's earlier one. The first line is "Quhen Merche wes with variand windis past."

8. Lewis, pp. 75–76.

9. Schipper, *Poems,* p. 93.

10. Lewis, p. 91.

11. The daisy is another flower associated with love and marriage, as may be seen in Chaucer's Alceste in the Prologue to the *Legend of Good Women.*

12. *To the Merchantis of Edinburgh,* title from Laing.

13. *To Aberdein,* (title apparently Mackenzie's own), ll. 1–8.

14. *Of Sir Thomas Norny,* title from Laing, based apparently on Pinkerton. See F. B. Snyder, "*Sir Thomas Nornay* and *Sir Thopas,*" *Modern Language Notes* 25 (1910), 78–80; and Elizabeth R. Eddy, "Sir Thopas and Sir Thomas Norny: Romance Parody in Chaucer and Dunbar," *Review of English Studies* 22 (1971), 401–9.

15. Eddy maintains that the *Sir* was probably part of the joke, pp. 406–7; cf. Baxter, pp. 129–30.

16. See, e.g., Mackay, STS, I, cix–cxii; Schipper, *Poems*, pp. 140–41; Janet Smith, *French Background*, pp. 51–57; and Ridley, p. 1009. Dunbar's flyting is apparently the earliest example of the form in Scots; its title comes from the Bannatyne manuscript.

17. Scott, p. 175.

18. Ibid., p. 178.

19. Mackay, STS, I, cxiii–cxiv.

20. On the Scottish imitations of the poem, see Gregor, STS, III, 36–37; and Janet Smith, *French Background*, pp. 51–52. See also John Skelton's *Against Garnesche* (ca. 1514), apparently his side of a flyting.

21. See Small, *Poems*, STS, II, 11.

22. See Mackay, STS, I, cxii. The main difference is in patterns of rhyme. After the initial challenge, the stanzas in Dunbar's speech rhyme *a b a b b c b c*, whereas those in Kennedy's speech continue the *a b a b b c c b* pattern found elsewhere in the poem.

23. Schipper, feeling that the organization of the poem as it has come down to us is "wholly confused," rearranged the stanzas into six parts, making an order that is more logical and chronological (*Poems*, pp. 144–49). But interesting as this reordering may be, it cannot be justified by any of the early texts of the poem. The versions in Bannatyne and Maitland, except at one point where stanzas in Maitland are displaced, show close agreement, as does the Chepman and Myllar print, which preserves the poem from line 316 to the end. See the criticism of this revision in Mackenzie, *Poems*, p. 198. There likewise seems to be no justification for Schipper's statement that from the "whole content" of the *Flyting*, it is evident that the different parts of it were written at intervals (*Poems*, p. 144).

24. See Small, *Poems*, STS, II, 29.

25. These stanzas may be rendered into Modern English, with difficulty, as follows: "Loon like Mahoun, get ready to obey me, / thief, or in grief mischief shall take you; / cry grace, dog face, or I will chase and slay you; / owl, roar and yowl, I shall defile your pride; / stripped hawk, both fed and bred at bitch's side, / and like a dog, pickpurse, that's what man thinks of you! / Scolded, impotent, covered with excrement, tanned hide, / climber of ladder, defiler of gallows, fowl adder, I defy you. / Chewed mutton, bitten excrement, peeled glutton, heir to Hillhous; / rank beggar, oyster dredger, foul flatterer in the inner house; / chitterling, rough rawhide shoe, like a shell in the mill house; / hateful bard, thief by nature, false traitor, offspring of fiends; / lump of tallow, gallows bird, cry defeat, you are overcome; / sheep driver, mealstore thief, whore-swiver, may misfortune fall on you: / heretic, lunatic, pickpurse, old woman's pet, / rotten old ewe, dirty ass, cry defeat, or I will kill you."

26. Baxter, p. 164. The title is based on the colophon in the Maitland manuscript.

27. "How she is protruding-mouthed like an ape, / and like a toad with

open mouth; / and how her short cat nose up turns; / and how she shines like soap; / my lady with the large lips. / When she is clad in rich apparel, / she shines as bright as a tar barrel; / when she was born, the sun suffered eclipse, / the night gladly fought on her behalf; / my lady with the large lips."

28. Shakespeare, *Sonnets* no. 127, 130. See also the various uncomplimentary references to the Moor Othello by other characters in the play.

29. Scott offers an evaluation of this poem wholly in accord with modern sentiments. He sees it showing the "barbarity" of James's court, "not only in the fact of the cruel enslaving of a negress as an object of amusement, but in the fact that Dunbar could write such a poem about her for a court audience. It is brutally inhuman and insensitive, the humour unworthy of civilised persons, and the skill of the poet merely bringing out the cruelty underlying the poem" (p. 68). In a footnote Scott adds that "Dunbar's conscious purpose of course is to burlesque the romance tradition tournament; but his bad taste is still scunnersome" (ibid.) This last Scots word almost makes this criticism tolerable.

30. Ridley, p. 1025. Instead of Andro the Maitland manuscript reads Walter, but Bannatyne, along with Chepman and Myllar, reads Andro. Bannatyne, however, states in its colophon that the poem was "maid by Dunbar quhen he [i.e., Kennedy] wes lyk to dy." See Small, *Poems*, STS, II, 58. Such a literal understanding of the piece by Bannatyne may make its authority suspect.

31. "Now I make my testament, / I leave my soul forevermore, / through all-powerful God, / in my lord's wine cellar; / there to remain forever, / until Doomsday without being removed, / good wine to drink, / with sweet Cuthbert that loved me never."

32. Villon also wrote a *Petit Testament*. An anonymous French poem of the time that may have influenced Dunbar is the *Testament de Tastvin roy des Pions*, a title freely translated by Mackenzie as "King of the Topers" (p. 213). Such poems may also be related to the ironic confessions of the medieval Goliardic poets, like the famous twelfth-century *Confessio* of the Archpoet.

33. Cf. the view of Mackay that Dunbar used Kennedy "to express his own freethinking mood and to say things he did not like to say in his own person" (STS, I, xcviii); echoed by Schipper, p. 210.

34. See especially Baxter, pp. 140–41; see also Mackay, STS, I, cxiv.

35. See Mackay, STS, I, ccxiv–ccxvi.

36. *The Fenyeit Freir of Tungland* (title from Hailes); *The Birth of Antichrist* (title from Laing); Damian's flight may also be alluded to in *Of Discretioun in Geving* (no. 15), ll. 36–37.

37. Rigg, pp. 269–73. Bryan S. Hay correctly points out that in these poems Dunbar was "concerned with matters larger than the mere degrading of one man" and that he "illustrates what happens when someone oper-

ates by a code of deception and makes 'feigning' the guiding principle of his life" ("William Dunbar's Flying Abbot: Apocalypse Made to Order," *Studies in Scottish Literature* 11 [1974], 217, 222).

38. On details here of Merlin, see J. A. W. Bennett, "Dunbar's *Birth of Antichrist*, 31–2," *Medium Aevum* 26 (1957), 196.

39. Ridley writes that "Whether the ladies are 'soliciting' in a court of justice or that of the king is not clear; possibly both" (p. 1030). The usual title, *Of the Ladyis Solistaris at Court,* following the colophon in the Redpeith Manuscript, suggests this ambiguity.

40. *Tydingis fra the Sessioun,* title from Ramsay. Although this Court was abolished in 1503–4, its replacement, the Court of Daily Council, was also called the Session (Ridley, p. 1026).

41. See, e.g., Ridley, p. 1025.

42. Scott, who takes Dunbar's various petitions to the king at face value, finds this "strange advice" indeed for the poet to be offering: "That Dunbar himself may have tried to live by these precepts is possible: that he failed to do so is evidenced by poem after poem in which he breaks most of his own rules. The poem may be a piece of quite innocent hypocrisy" (p. 155).

43. *Aganis the Solistaris in Court,* title from the colophon in Maitland, not to be confused with *Of the Lady Solistaris at Court,* no. 48.

44. Schipper (citing Pinkerton), *Poems,* p. 44.

45. *Remonstrance to the King,* title from Laing. Ridley writes that the two poems together give "a striking picture of the court of James IV" (p. 1013).

46. "Feigners, hypocrites, and flatterers; / cryers, boasters and chatterers; / murmurers, grumblers, shifty-eyed characters, and babblers."

47. These two poems may also be related, especially in terms of subject and method, to "Complane I wald, wist I quhome till" (no. 19). cf. nos. 11 and 12.

48. Baxter, p. 51.

49. The title *To the Quene* was first given by Pinkerton.

50. The sheep imagery may come about, as Scott suggests, because of the possible meaning of "pockis" as sheep rot (pp. 164–65). After analyzing the poem for three pages Scott dismisses it, saying that it is "not worth the energy spent on construing it, being an inferior and distasteful thing though morally serious enough under the jocularity" (p. 165).

51. Baxter, p. 58.

52. See also the *Venus Mass* attributed to Lydgate and the noteworthy thirteenth-century *Messe des Oiseaux* by Jean de Condé.

53. See, e.g., Kurt Wittig, *The Scottish Tradition in Literature* (Edinburgh, 1958), p. 57.

54. Matt. 4:2–4; Luke 4:2–4.

55. Luke 1:26 ff.

Chapter Four

1. See nos. 14–16, and nos. 67, 69, 70.
2. Scott. p. 320: see the list here.
3. See, e.g., the section in Mackenzie, *Poems*, p. ix; echoed in Ridley, pp. 1040 ff.
4. *Of the Warldis Vanitie*, title from Laing. Schipper, who calls this poem "one of the finest of Dunbar's religious poems," uses it as the concluding poem of his edition (*Poems*, p. 386).
5. *Of Manis Mortalitie*, title from Laing, based on Hailes.
6. In *English Lyrics of the XIIIth Century*, ed. Carleton Brown (Oxford, 1932), no. 81; cf. no. 52.
7. On number symbolism in general and on the various biblical uses of 40 in terms of trial and privation in particular, see Vincent F. Hopper, *Medieval Number Symbolism. Its Sources. Meaning, and Influence on Thought and Expression* (New York, 1938), esp. pp. 15, 26, 71.
8. *Advice to Spend Anis Awin Gude*, title from Hailes.
9. *Ane His Awin Ennemy*, title from Hailes.
10. No. 2. ll. 21–22. Schipper, however, sees a "humorous tone" in this poem (*Poems*, p. 40). See also nos. 67, 69, 70.
11. No. 67 (*Of Covetyce*), ll. 41–43.
12. *Of Deming*, title from Hailes.
13. *How Sall I Governe Me?* title from Laing.
14. Tucker, *Verse Satire*, p. 136; Smith calls him "a satirist with a distinction. He is neither the stern preacher like Langland, nor the spiteful accuser like Lyndsay. His verse is more akin to the quipping manner of Chaucer" (*Transition*, p. 54). It seems incredible that Wittig can write, however, that none of Dunbar's poems is "in the strict sense satirical, for Dunbar uses no moral yardstick" (p. 72).
15. *A General Satyre*, title from Ramsay. Whereas Bannatyne cites Dunbar as author of this work, Maitland ascribes it to Sir James Inglis, not known for any other writings. This attribution is, however, supported by Mackenzie, *Poems*, pp. 224–25; see the discussion in Schipper, *Poems*, pp. 311–13; and cf. Ridley, who feels that the grounds for removing the poem from the Dunbar canon are inadequate (p. 1045).
16. See *The Complete Poems of John Skelton, Laureate*, ed. Philip Henderson, 2d ed. (London, 1948), p. 133.
17. Scott feels that the verse form is too intricate "to permit a very deep view of the subject so that the theme becomes a mere catalogue with insufficient comment" (pp. 321–22).
18. *The Devillis Inquest*, title from Laing, perhaps based on title in Asloan MS.
19. The poem exists in quite different forms in Bannatyne and Maitland; see the discussion in Mackenzie, *Poems*, pp. 238–39; and Baxter, pp. 112,

238–39. Schipper calls the poem "a powerful satire on the manners of the time" (*Poems*, p. 81).

20. Tucker, p. 141. The title, *The Dance of the Sevin Deidly Synnis*, is from Laing.

21. As may be seen in the *Life of Schir William Wallace* by Blind Harry the Minstrel, however, Macfadden is the enemy of the Scottish hero, Wallace (VII, 627 ff); see Mackay, STS, I, ccxliii–iv.

22. Scott, p. 231; cf. Speirs, pp. 61–62.

23. In Maitland, followed by the STS edition, the poem is organized entirely in six-line stanzas.

24. See Ridley, p. 1035.

25. *The Sowtar and Tailyouris War*, title from colophon in Maitland. The term "war" is misleading, and, though followed by Mackenzie, other editions use the more accurate term "tournament" or "joust." Here the poem will henceforth be referred to as the *Tournament*.

26. Baxter suggests that the *Dance* may be a literary counterpart of the carnival scenes, or composed for recitation as part of the Tuesday revelry (p. 154).

27. Mackay suggests that it "may be a satirical account of an actual occurrence" (STS, I, c). See also Allan H. Maclaine, "The *Christis Kirk* Tradition: Its Evolution in Scots Poetry to Burns," *Studies in Scottish Literature* 2 (1964), 16–18.

28. Baxter, p. 158.

29. Mackay, STS, I, c; see also Tucker, p. 140.

30. Chaucer, for instance, to get at the "condicioun" of his Canterbury pilgrims, describes their garb (A 38–41). More particularly, see, e.g., Shakespeare's words in *King Lear:* "You cowardly rascal, nature disclaims in thee: / a tailor made thee" (II, ii, 54–55). See also Scott, p. 238.

31. Ed. Small, *Poems*, STS, II, 128.

32. Title from Pinkerton.

33. See Ridley, p. 1028.

34. Scott, p. 65.

35. See e.g., the classification in Mackenzie, *Poems*, p.viii.

36. Schipper, *Poems*, p. 72.

37. Wittig, p. 73.

38. Kinsley (*Poems*, pp. 77–78) gives a version different from that in Mackenzie; but according to my reading, he is wrong to have the speaker in stanza 4 the same as the one in stanza 3; though cf. Baxter, p. 56, n.

39. Baxter calls it "an indoor counterpart" of the *Tretis* (p. 56).

40. Schipper calls this piece, whose title comes from Laing, "little else" than portions of Chaucer's *Parson's Tale* put into verse (*Poems*, p. 354).

41. The reading in the Redpeith manuscript, the only text of this poem, has been taken as "freindlie"; but this, as Scott realizes, can hardly be correct, though Schipper had translated the "freindlie fantasie" as "a pleas-

ant vision," that is, "one tempting the senses" and "sent by the Devil" (*Poems*, p. 243). Scott suggests that the word should be "feindlie" (p. 151), and as far as sense is concerned, this is better than "freindlie," though it involves ignoring an *r* clearly in the text. The emendation suggested here, "fremdlie," is a word that existed in the North of England from the late fourteenth century through at least the fifteenth century (see *Middle English Dictionary*, III, 883) and could easily have been misread as "freindlie" if the downstrokes of the *m* were confused with the letters *in*.

42. Schipper's identification of "Schir Bet-the-Kirk" with the king hardly seems likely (*Poems*, p. 246).

43. Scott, p. 151.

44. On "inoportunitie" as a possible error for "importunitie," see *Middle English Dictionary*, V, 207.

45. See ibid., V, 109; also Dunbar's disapproving reference to "innopportoun askaris" in "Schir, ye have mony servitouris," no. 17, l. 43. Schipper glosses the term as "want of fitness" (*Poems*, p. 486).

46. Scott, however, feels that its "mixture of conventions" is unsatisfactory, and that "the allegorical machinery is too cumbersome for the subject." His conclusion is that "The poem is more of a curiosity than an achievement" (pp. 153–54).

47. *Of the Passioun of Christ*, title from Laing.

48. Scott, p. 286.

49. Schipper, *Poems*, p. 375.

50. *Of the Changes of Lyfe*, title from Pinkerton.

51. Ridley, p. 1045.

52. According to Wittig, "the spirit of Dunbar's religious poetry is essentially liturgical and expresses the formula of religion," a generality he uses the *Orisoun* (title from Laing) to illustrate (p. 56).

53. Lewis, p. 95; cf. Ridley's view of it as "a conventional Nativity lyric" (p. 1046).

54. Scott, p. 183.

55. Ridley, p. 1047. The title of the poem is from Hailes. Perhaps for rhyme, "force" in l. 2 should be something like "foes."

56. Baxter, p. 214.

57. Smith, *Transition*, p. 51.

58. Douglas Gray, *Themes and Images in the Medieval English Religious Lyric* (London, 1972), p. 148.

59. Lewis, p. 96.

60. A list of some of these may be found in *Medieval English Lyrics: A Critical Anthology*, ed. R. T. Davies (London, 1963), p. 359. See also the valuable article by Isabel Hyde, "Primary Sources and Associations of Dunbar's Aureate Imagery," *Modern Language Review* 51 (1956), 481–92.

61. It may be significant that here the images describing Satan are in the form of metaphors, whereas those describing Christ take the form of similes.

62. *Ane Ballat of Our Lady*, title from Laing.

63. Baxter, p. 213.

64. Ridley, pp. 1047–48; she also described it as "largely a repetitious heaping up of praise of Mary."

65. Scott, p. 304.

66. Janet Smith feels that the poem shows "a mixture of two styles, the old style of the Latin hymns, and the new elaboration of the French *Rhétoriqueurs*" (*French Background*, p. 75).

67. "Hail, star on high! Hail, in eternity, / shining in sight of God! / Lamp in darkness discerning / by glory and divine grace; / of today, now and forever, / queen of angels! / Our troubles below to drive away, / help, most royal rose. / Hail, Mary, full of grace! / Hail, fresh flower of women! / Desire us, govern us, maternal virgin, / of pity both root and bark."

68. *The Tabill of Confession*, title from Laing. The colophon in Maitland, "Heir endis ane Confessioun generale compylit be Maister Williame Dunbar," probably provides the best title. See Small, *Poems*, STS, II, 71.

69. This is what Scott seems to do when he questions whether some of the sins confessed are really pertinent to Dunbar, p. 290.

70. *Canterbury Tales*, X 46–51.

Chapter Five

1. Scott, p. 40.

2. *Gude Counsale*, title from Laing.

3. Baxter refers to their "wordly advice, concerned with the need for keeping up social appearances" (p. 195). Cf. Schipper, who wants to relate the poem's advice to that in *Rewl of Anis Self*, no. 41 (*Poems*, p. 324).

4. Ridley, p. 1041.

5. *Quhone He List to Feyne*, title from Laing, based on Bannatyne.

6. Small, *Poems*, STS, II, 246.

7. Schipper, *Poems*, p. 110.

8. Ridley, p. 1030; even Scott recognizes this as a "humorous poem" (pp. 59–60).

9. Scott, p. 60.

10. Ridley, p. 1031.

11. See *Middle English Dictionary*, II, 991, 994; also *Dictionary of the Older Scottish Tongue*, II, 84.

12. The variant "lad" is listed in both the *Middle English Dictionary*, V, 1243–44; and the *Dictionary of the Older Scottish Tongue*, III, 578.

13. *To a Ladye*, title from Pinkerton.

14. See, e.g., Mackay, STS, III, 307; and Ridley, p. 1030.

15. If this were the case, the poem "would not then be a love-poem but a petition for advancement" (Baxter, p. 121).

16. Scott, p. 58.

17. Speirs, p. 58.

18. On rue, see esp. *Batman vppon Bartholome, De Proprietatibus*

Rerum (London, 1582), XVII, cxli. Scott suggests that the reference to the killing of rue by "Merche, with his caild blastis keyne" (11) might actually be to Dunbar himself, who was perhaps related to the earls of March (see *Flyting*, l. 262; Scott, pp. 58–59).

19. Scott, pp. 57–58.

20. The title, from Laing, is most likely based on the last line of the poem. The mid-sixteenth-century *Compleynt of Scotland* refers to a song, one of the "sueit sangis of Scotland," "Lady, help 3our Presoneir," that has been taken as this poem (see Mackay, STS, III, 253; Ridley, p. 1033). More likely, however, given the length and un-songlike nature of this poem, both it and the song are to be seen as manifestations of the same popular convention.

21. Schipper, *Poems*, p. 113.

22. Scott, p. 53. In Bannatyne the poem is anonymous; in Redpeith the first two stanzas appear and are ascribed to Dunbar.

23. This may be defined as "the lady's assessment of how far the lover falls short of the ideal" (Kinsley, *Poems*, p. 113).

24. Scott, p. 52.

25. Ridley, pp. 1032–33.

26. Baxter, p. 105. Baxter finds attempts to connect the poem with James IV and Margaret Drummond mere speculations (p. 106); cf. Mackay, STS, I, lxxix, clx.

27. Title from Chepman and Myllar.

28. Scott, p. 40.

29. Speirs, p. 56.

30. Lines 17–18, ed. Small, EETS, p. 223.

31. Lewis, p. 92; see also Wittig, p. 66.

32. Fox, "Dunbar's *The Golden Targe*," ELH 26 (1959), 318. Walter Scheps insists that in its "willful juxtaposition of brilliance and incompetance," the poem "reflects and calls attention to the inconsistencies of the genre of allegorical love-vision" ("*The Goldyn Targe*: Dunbar's Comic Psychomachia," *Papers on Language and Literature* 11 [1975], 353).

33. Fox, pp. 317–18.

34. Ibid., pp. 331–32; see also pp. 320–21. This idea has recently been developed by Lois A. Ebin, "The Theme of Poetry in Dunbar's 'Goldyn Targe,' " *Chaucer Review* 7 (1972), 147–59; see also Frank Shuffelton, who, while making a good case for the poem's being part of an entertainment for Bernard Stewart in 1508, shows that Dunbar and his audience were interested in "the process of fabrication, the technology of language" ("An Imperial Flower: Dunbar's *The Golden Targe* and the Court Life of James IV of Scotland," *Studies in Philology* 72 [1975], 205).

35. Fox, p. 330; cf. Roderick J. Lyall, who feels that the poem is primarily about "the evils of an immediate concern with the pleasures of the senses" ("Moral Allegory in Dunbar's 'Golden Targe,' " *Studies in Scottish Literature* 11 [1973], 65).

36. Fox, p. 334. On the meanings of images and mythological references in the poem, see E. Allen Tilley, "The Meaning of Dunbar's 'The Golden Targe,' " *Studies in Scottish Literature* 10 (1973), 220–31.

37. "Finally, like one recovering from an illness, a mental breakdown, the poet rediscovers the actual world and real May morning in the real garden" (Scott, p. 44).

38. For Fox, "Enamel is clear and brilliant, colorful, with a rich sweet beauty, and, most particularly, is a surface adornment, like illumination, flowers, and gold or sugar coating" (p. 333). On light as a principal symbol in the poem for good writing, see Fox, pp. 332–34.

39. *Inconstancy of Luve*, title from Laing.

40. Sometimes this poem is entitled *Ane Brash of Wooing*, following Ramsay.

41. Line 23 in Mackenzie, *Poems*, reads "my tuchan and my calfe," with "tuchan"—his emendation—meaning "a calf's skin stuffed with straw, to encourage the cow to give milk" (Kinsley, *Poems*, p. 118). The term in Maitland is "cuchair," in Bannatyne "cowffyne." Whereas "cuchair" could be a form of "couchour," from Old French "couchan," meaning a kind of spaniel (see *Middle English Dictionary*, I, 643), the more likely meaning comes from the root "cu-" or "cow-," both suggesting the bovine. The main trouble with Mackenzie's emendation is that "tuchan" destroys the alliteration of the line. The "cow" morpheme is probably the reason for the inclusion of "cowhubye" in l. 58.

42. Though usually glossed as capercaillie or wood-grouse, its association here with "kyd" may suggest that the "capir-" root was taken from Latin "caper," meaning goat, as in "Capricorn," of which "capirculyoun" might be a development.

43. Honey references appear also in ll. 1, 30, 39.

44. Besides referring to clover and ribwort plantain (Kinsley, *Poems*, p. 143) or sugar plum (Schipper, *Poems*, p. 38), the terms may also mean "cleaver" and "curl-cutter."

45. See, e.g., Chaucer's *Troilus and Criseyde*, II, 585, 1087; III, 1371; V, 549.

46. Schipper, following Jamieson in the *Etymological Dictionary of the Scottish Language*, glosses "crowdie mowdie" as "Milk and meal boiled together" (*Poems*, p. 39).

47. *The Merle and the Nychtingaill*, title from Laing, though perhaps based on the Asloan manuscript. Hailes and Pinkerton call it *The Twa Luves Erdly and Devyne*. See Mackay, STS, III, 263.

48. Scott, p. 280.

49. Schipper, however, feels that "the heart of the poet" favors the view of the merle (*Poems*, p. 346).

50. *Of Luve Erdly and Divine*, title from Hailes.

51. See Baxter's criticism of such a view (p. 98).

52. Scott, p. 277.

53. Schipper, *Poems*, pp. 345–46, 351.

54. Ridley, p. 1031.

55. See also Dunbar's *Thrissil and the Rois,* no. 55, l. 12.

56. *In Prais of Wemen*, title from Laing.

57. See the discussion in Baxter, p. 57.

58. Schipper, *Poems*, p. 76; Schipper, however, classifies the piece under "Satirical Poems against the Female Sex."

59. Scott, p. 56.

60. Ridley, p. 1028.

61. Title from Maitland.

62. Ridley, p. 1029.

63. Baxter, p. 53; see also Wittig, p. 72.

64. Speirs, p. 58.

65. Lewis, p. 94.

66. Scott, p. 202.

67. See A. D. Hope, *A Midsummer Eve's Dream: Variations on a Theme by William Dunbar* (Canberra, 1970), pp. 10, 14–15.

68. H. Harvey Wood, *Two Scots Chaucerians,* Writers and Their Work, 201 (London, 1967), pp. 42–43.

69. Speirs, p. 60.

70. Kinsley, *Poems*, p. xvii; repr. from "The *Tretis of the twa mariit wemen and the wedo,*" *Medium Aevum* 22 (1954), esp. 35.

71. Kinsley, *Poems*, p. xvi.

72. On the relationship of the poem to this traditional genre, see Janet Smith, *French Background*, pp. 38–41.

73. Lewis, p. 94.

74. Although Kinsley notes that such a contrast is at the center of the poem, for him the contrast is "between the ideal world of courtly poetry and the 'spotted actuality' of the three women's minds and habits" (*Poems*, p. xviii).

75. Hope gives a good translation of the entire poem facing the original from Mackenzie's edition (pp. 270–99). He renders these lines as follows: "I have a slack sloven, a worm, an old crawly caterpillar, / a worn-out boar good for nothing but clap-trap; / a bumbler, a drone bee, a bag full of phlegm; / a scabby scrag, a scorpion, a poop-bum" (p. 275).

76. Lewis, p. 94.

77. As Hope suggests, Midsummer's Eve and Halloween were related in the Middle Ages and in the old Scottish calendar, marking the midpoint and end of the year (p. 16).

78. Ibid., pp. 11, 16.

79. Ibid., pp. 18–23.

80. On the proper and usual ways of celebrating Midsummer's Eve, see ibid., p. 24.

81. For an argument about the possibility of the scene's suggesting fer-

tility rites, and on the relationship of this to the impotence continually cited by the women, see ibid., pp. 22–23.

82. Jacobus de Voragine, *The Golden Legend,* trans. William Caxton, (London, 1900), V, 70.

Chapter Six

1. In *"Rorate celi desuper"* (no. 79) this linking of audience and poet comes through the Latin refrain, "Et nobis puer natus est," to us a child is born.

2. See also, e.g., no. 2, l. 25; no. 51, l. 15; no. 53, l. 19; no. 67, l. 41.

3. This poem is sometimes called *Dunbar at Oxinfurde* because of a colophon in Maitland, but nothing in the poem is about Oxford, and the name does not even appear in the poem.

4. Line 11; see also l. 26.

5. Ridley, p. 1008.

6. Title from Pinkerton.

7. Plays may perhaps mean comic poems, not dramas, but at the same time we must recognize that the speaker here is not necessarily the poet.

8. Gray, *Themes and Images*, p. 218.

9. No. 66, ll. 18–20.

10. See Ridley, p. 1010.

11. Schipper, p. 328.

12. See in particular the use of "Thare saw I" constructions in the *Goldyn Targe*, esp. ll. 73–126.

13. Morgan, "Dunbar and the Language of Poetry," p. 156.

14. "You Lazarus, you loathly, emaciated, rotting corpse, / to all the world you may be an example, / to look upon your grisly, pitiful face, / for your eye is hideous, discolored, and hollow; / your cheek-bone is bare, and your complexion is pallid; / your jaw, your jowel, cause men to remain chaste; / your throat makes us think that we must die: / I exorcise you, you hungry, Highland spirit."

15. See esp. ll. 17–40.

16. Scott, p. 306. See esp. the analysis of Dunbar's versification by Scott, pp. 306–31; and by G. P. M'Neill in STS, I, clxxii–cxciii.

17. Scott, p. 318.

18. Nos. 1–2, 8–9, 12, 14–16, 20–21, 31, 37, 42, 46, 69–70.

19. Nos. 3, 10–11, 25, and 66 are in tetrameter; nos. 4, 39, 49, and 60 are in pentameter, while no. 77, also in pentameter, uses a refrain.

20. Identical to these two poems in stanzaic form and number of lines is "Sanct Salvatour! send silver sorrow" (no. 1), and while this seems close to "Madam, your men" in its imagery and humor, it may represent still another variation of content and theme.

21. Nos. 7, 13, 18, 23–24, 33–34, 59, 67, 71–72.

22. Nos. 41, 53, 61–64, 68, 73, 75, 78, 81, 83; also no. 65, if it is by Dunbar.

23. E.g., ll. 233–48; 545–52.

24. *Testament of the Papyngo*, ll. 17–18, ed. Small, EETS, p. 223.

Selected Bibliography

PRIMARY SOURCES

1. Manuscripts and Early Printings

Chepman and Myllar Prints. Edinburgh, 1508. Edited by G. Stevenson. Scottish Text Society 12. Edinburgh: Blackwood, 1918. Photofacsimile, edited by William Beattie. Edinburgh: Bibliographical Society, 1950. Contains six poems by Dunbar.

Asloan Manuscript (ca. 1515). Auchinleck, Ayrshire. Edited by W. A. Craigie. Scottish Text Society 16–17. Vols. 1–2. Edinburgh: Blackwood, 1924. Badly damaged manuscript; in present state contains three poems by Dunbar and part of a fourth.

Bannatyne Manuscript (ca. 1568). Edinburgh; National Library of Scotland. Edited by W. Tod Ritchie. Scottish Text Society 22–23. Vols. 2–3. Edinburgh: Blackwood, 1928. Contains sixty poems by Dunbar.

Maitland Folio Manuscript (ca. 1570–86). Pepysian Library, Magdalene College, Cambridge. Edited by W. A. Craigie. Scottish Text Society 7. Vol. 1. Edinburgh: Blackwood, 1919. Contains sixty-one poems attributed to Dunbar.

Redpeith Manuscript (1622–23). Cambridge University Library. Mainly a copy of Maitland, contains forty-seven poems by Dunbar, twelve of which are printed in vol. 2 of Craigie edition of Maitland Folio, STS 20 (1927), pp. 40–58.

2. Modern Editions

The Poems of William Dunbar. Edited by John Small; Introduction and appendices by A. J. G. Mackay, and notes by W. Gregor and Mackay. Scottish Text Society 2, 4, 16, 21, 29. 3 Vols. Edinburgh: Blackwood, 1883–93. Contains fullest annotations and glossary.

The Poems of William Dunbar. Edited by J. Schipper. 5 parts. Vienna: Kaiserliche Akademie der Wissenschaften, 1891–94. Gives most textual variants, written in English.

The Poems of William Dunbar. Edited by W. Mackay Mackenzie. London: Faber and Faber, 1932; repr. 1960, with corrections by Bruce Dickins. Standard available text.

173

William Dunbar. Poems. Edited by James Kinsley. Clarendon Medieval and Tudor Series. Oxford: Clarendon Press, 1958. Fair selection of poems.

SECONDARY SOURCES

1. General Studies

FOX, DENTON. "The Scottish Chaucerians." In *Chaucer & Chaucerians: Critical Studies in Middle English Literature*, ed. D. S. Brewer. University, Ala.: University of Alabama Press, 1966. Pp. 164–200, esp. pp. 179–87. Excellent introductory study.

KINGHORN, A. M. "The Mediaeval Makars." *Texas Studies in Literature and Language* 1 (1959), 73–88. Good comparison-contrast of major Scottish poets from Henryson to Lindsay.

KINSLEY, JAMES. "The Mediaeval Makars." In *Scottish Poetry: A Critical Survey*. London: Cassell and Conpey, 1955. Esp. pp. 24–32. Brief but perceptive study.

LEWIS, C. S. "The Close of the Middle Ages in Scotland." in *English Literature in the Sixteenth Century, Excluding Drama*. Oxford: Clarendon Press, 1954, esp. pp. 90–100. Important and influential study.

SMITH, G. GREGORY. "The Scottish Poets." in *The Trasition Period*. Edinburgh: Blackwood, 1900. Pp. 35–84, esp. pp. 48–58. Perceptive criticism, still valuable.

SMITH, JANET M. "Dunbar." In *The French Background of Middle Scots Literature*. Edinburgh: Oliver and Boyd, 1934, pp. 60–77. Good assessment of influence, showing it to be more general than particular.

SPEIRS, JOHN. "William Dunbar." In *The Scots Literary Tradition: An Essay in Criticism*. 2d ed. London: Faber and Faber, 1962. Pp. 54–68. Vague and impressionistic criticism, essentially a reprint of article in *Scrutiny* 7 (1938), 56–68.

WITTIG, KURT. "The Makars: William Dunbar." in *The Scottish Tradition in Literature*. Edinburgh: Oliver and Boyd, 1958. Esp. pp. 53–76. Uneven general study, at times useful.

WOOD, H. HARVEY. "William Dunbar." In *Two Scots Chaucerians*. Writers and Their Work 201. London: Longmans, Green, 1967. Pp. 23–44. Unexciting survey.

2. Bibliography

GEDDIE, WILLIAM. *A Bibliography of Middle Scots Poets*. Scottish Text Society 61. Edinburgh Blackwood, 1912. Esp. pp. 187–222.

RIDLEY, FLORENCE H. "Middle Scots Writers." In *A Manual of the Writings in Middle English, 1050–1500*, Vol. 4, ed. Albert E. Hartung. New Haven: Connecticut Academy of Arts and Sciences, 1973. Esp. pp. 1005–60, 1204–84. Most up-to-date coverage of Dunbar; see also

Ridley, *Studies in Scottish Literature* 8 (1970), esp. 44–51; and Peter Heidtmann, *Chaucer Review* 5 (1970), 55–82.

3. Books

BAXTER, J.W. *William Dunbar: A Biographical Study.* Edinburgh: Oliver and Boyd, 1952. More valuable for its critical assessments than for its biographical details; see review by Matthew P. McDiarmid, *Scottish Historical Review* 33 (1954), 46–52.

HOPE, A.D. *A Midsummer Eve's Dream: Variations on a Theme by William Dunbar.* Camberra: Australian National University Press, 1970. Unusual study focussing on the *Tretis of the Tua Mariit Wemen and the Wedo*, emphasizing its place in folklore and legend, with translation of poem; of limited value.

SCHIPPER, J. *William Dunbar: Sein Leben und seine Gedichte.* Berlin: Trübner, 1884. Fanciful biography but useful critical commentary.

SCOTT, TOM. *Dunbar: A Critical Exposition of the Poems.* Edinburgh: Oliver and Boyd, 1966. Subjective and long-winded; marred by author's viewing Dunbar in terms of his own social and economic preferences.

4. Articles

BAWCUTT, PRISCILLA. "Aspects of Dunbar's Imagery." In *Chaucer and Middle English Studies in Honour of Rossell Hope Robbins.* Kent, Oh.: Kent State University Press, 1974. Pp. 190–200. Valuable study of Dunbar's imagery in noncourtly and nonreligious poems.

DORSCH, T.S. "Of Discretioun in Asking: Dunbar's Petitionary Poems." In *Chaucer und seine Zeit: Symposion für Walter F. Schirmer.* Buchreihe der Anglia 14. Tübingen: Max Niemeyer, 1968. Pp. 285–92. Of limited interest.

EBIN, LOIS A. "The Theme of Poetry in Dunbar's 'Goldyn Targe.'" *Chaucer Review* 7 (1972), 147–59. On relationship between poet and his matter.

EDDY, ELIZABETH R. "Sir Thopas and Sir Thomas Norny: Romance Parody in Chaucer and Dunbar." *Review of English Studies* 22 (1971), 401–9. Includes full comparison of the two poems.

FOX, DENTON. "The Chronology of William Dunbar." *Philological Quarterly* 39 (1960), 413–25. Pertinent study of biography and canon.

———. "Dunbar's *The Golden Targe.*" *ELH* 26 (1959), 211–34. Good analysis emphasizing Dunbar's artistry.

HAY, BRYAN S. "William Dunbar's Flying Abbot: Apocalypse Made to Order" *Studies in Scottish Literature* 11 (1974), 217–25. On thematic concerns of the *Birth of Antichrist* and the *Fenyeit Friar.*

HYDE, ISABEL. "Poetic Imagery: A Point of Comparison between Henryson and Dunbar." *Studies in Scottish Literature* 2 (1964–65), 183–97. Good stylistic study emphasizing differences between the two poets.

————. "Primary Sources and Associations of Dunbar's Aureate Imagery." *Modern Language Review* 51 (1956), 481–92. Valuable study of basis of Dunbar's religious imagery in Bible, liturgy, and exegetical commentaries.

JACK, RONALD D. S. "Dunbar and Lydgate." *Studies in Scottish Literature* 8 (1970–71), 215–27. Study of influence, especially on *Goldyn Targe*.

KINGHORN, A. M. "Dunbar and Villon—A Comparison and a Contrast." *Modern Language Review* 62 (1967), 195–208. Good study of differences between the two poets.

LEYERLE, JOHN. "The Two Voices of William Dunbar." *University of Toronto Quarterly* 31 (1962), 316–38. Good study of aureate and eldritch voices.

LYALL, RODERICK J. "Moral Allegory in Dunbar's 'Golden Targe,' " *Studies in Scottish Literature* 11 (1973), 47–65. On poem's concern with the contrast between virtue and sexual love.

MACKENZIE, W. MACKAY. "William Dunbar." In *Edinburgh Essays on Scots Literature*. Edinburgh: Oliver and Boyd, 1933, pp. 27–55. General study, still somewhat useful.

MORGAN, EDWIN. "Dunbar and the Language of Poetry." *Essays in Criticism* 2 (1952), 138–58. Interesting general appreciation.

NICHOLS, P. H. "William Dunbar as a Scottish Lydgatian." *PMLA* 46 (1931), 214–24. Emphasizes aureate diction.

————. "Lydgate's Influence on the Aureate Terms of the Scottish Chaucerians." *PMLA* 47 (1932), 516–22.

RIGG, A. G. "William Dunbar: the 'Fenyeit Friar.' " *Review of English Studies* 14 (1963), 269–73. On theme of feigned friar as a literary device.

SCHEPS, WALTER. "*The Goldyn Targe*: Dunbar's Comic *Psychomachia*" *Papers on Language and Literature* 11 (1975), 339–56. Sees poem as essentially comic presentation of the conventions of the allegorical love-vision.

SHUFFELTON, FRANK. "An Imperial Flower: Dunbar's *The Golden Targe* and the Court Life of James IV of Scotland," *Studies in Philology* 72 (1975), 193–207. Good study of poem as court entertainment, as the verbal equivalent of spectacle.

SWART, J. "On Re-reading William Dunbar." In *Chaucer and Middle English Studies in Honour of Rossell Hope Robbins*. Kent, Oh.: Kent State University Press, 1974. Pp. 201–9. General appreciation.

TILLEY, E. ALLEN. "The Meaning of Dunbar's 'The Golden Targe." *Studies in Scottish Literature* 10 (1973), 220–31. Especially on tradition behind images.

Index